Mechanical Horses

Bill Aldridge

Inside front cover top

Because British Railway Scammell Scarab tractor units were so common during the 1950s and 60s, few people ever bothered to photograph them. The author was lucky enough to be sent a colour photograph of one working in Leeds and it is reproduced here.

Inside front cover lower

In Beverley in the East Riding of Yorkshire a pair of 6-ton Scammell Scarab tractor units commenced work in the mid-1960s for Barrow Hepburn Ltd. Amongst their many tasks was the movement of raw materials from the Beckside warehouse to the factory and the movement of finished product within the factory. Despite various changes of ownership, at least one Scarab was still working in 1985, a testament to the quality of workmanship shown by the workers at Watford.

Inside rear cover top

In Greenfield, near Oldham, Robert Fletcher Ltd operated a large paper mill and used a Scammell Scarab and this 1973 Leyland tractor unit as works transport. Both vehicles were fitted with 6-ton Scammell automatic couplings. The Leyland is seen here in 1991, still gainfully employed. The site was established as a paper mill in 1921, but ultimately became loss-making and closed in 2001.

Inside rear cover lower

Into the 1980s the main users of the automatic coupling system were the previously nationalised parcel carrying concerns of National Carriers (ex-British Railways Sundries Division) and Roadline (the parcels division of British Road Services).
For 8 to 10 ton loads the Ford D Series 1110 model was used as the basis for an automatic coupling tractor unit. This model was purchased by National Carriers and also by the railway-owned and operated Rail Express Parcels service. The NCL vehicle is seen in Grimsby.

Rear cover top

The Grimsby Ice Company operated 11 of the 6-ton capacity Scammell Mechanical Horses for the delivery of ice to trawlers and fish merchants within the Grimsby docks. All the Mechanical Horses were bought second hand from the Ministry of Supply in the late 1940s and most were later converted to battery traction. Built in 1900, the Grimsby Ice Company factory produced 1,500 tons of ice per day at its peak, but unfortunately closed in 1990 when fishing patterns changed. Seen here is the last operating 6-ton Mechanical Horse, photographed in 1980.

Rear cover lower

Amongst the many users were Firth Brown Steels in Sheffield where both 3 and 6-ton Scarabs were to be found operating within the steel works and a 3-ton Scarab dating from 1962 was still in good condition when photographed 18 years later.

Title Page

This photograph taken outside Watford's Isolation Hospital in Tolpits Lane, just down the road from the Scammell works, shows an early doorless 6-ton Mechanical Horse. Most 6-ton Mechanical Horses were fitted with a sloping windscreen and this horse is unusual in that it sports a vertical windscreen similar to the rather basic models supplied to the railway companies. Of particular interest are the tractor unit's side lights. These are mounted above the windscreen on stalks to enable them to be raised horizontally to show the ultimate width of the trailer, which was invariably wider than the horse.

This delightful photograph shows a Scammell 3-ton capacity Mechanical Horse operated jointly by the Great Western and London Midland & Scottish Railways, collecting, along with others, a consignment of umbrella sticks destined for 'Colonial Use''. The location is Bourne Mill near Stroud which at the time was owned by HS Hack Ltd. *(Courtesy Mr D Smith)*

Scammell
Mechanical Horse

3 & 6 TON MODELS
(M.H.3 & M.H.6)

INSTRUCTION BOOK

FIRST EDITION

SCAMMELL LORRIES LTD.
HIGH HOLBORN HOUSE, W.C.1

Telephone : Chancery 8333. Telegrams : "Twelfton, Holb. London."
Works and Service Station for London and Home Counties
WATFORD WEST, HERTS.

ILLUSTRATING MECHANICAL HORSE ON FULL LOCK SHOWING
EXCEPTIONALLY SMALL TURNING CIRCLE

PROTOTYPE COB 1930

The original Karrier Cob tractor unit was based on a slightly earlier rigid three-wheel load-carrying chassis. The small wheels were originally fitted to give a low loading height when the vehicle was used as a dustcart, but when the LMS Railway converted the model to a tractor unit, the small wheels made it possible to fit the front axle of a horse dray onto the tractor, thereby making an articulated unit as shown in this LNE Railway version, complete with sad looking brakesman for the trailer.

A slightly later modified Karrier Cob Junior model made use of a four-cylinder petrol engine, but retained the small solid tyres. The larger engine meant that the cab itself needed enlarging. This picture depicts one of these Cobs after an intermediate overhaul.

Introduction

This book is intended to cover an area of road transport history that has been given scant coverage in the published media. The subject is the introduction of articulation into the road haulage industry and its consequent rise to become the accepted form of transport for heavier loads. An articulated vehicle is one where the load-carrying portion of the vehicle, known as the trailer, is attached to the power unit, known as the tractor, by a coupling, which allows the two components to safely swivel in the horizontal and vertical modes. From the 1970s the fifth wheel coupling became the established means of coupling articulated tractor and trailer, yet the most common form of articulated coupling within the United Kingdom before that period was the automatic coupling designed by the ingenious Mr OD North of Scammell Lorries Ltd in the very early 1930s. It was a coupling system taken up enthusiastically by own-account operators as well as road hauliers. Yet, strangely enough, it was the railway companies who promoted the concept for use in their road collection and delivery operations.

To continue the story, it will describe why the automatic coupling system was designed, how it was popularised and why it was eventually to fall from favour. In addition, it will cover some interesting concepts that arose from the basic design. Although the majority of the text of this book is devoted to the products of the famous Watford factory of Scammell Lorries and their imitators, it is necessary to understand where the concept of 'automatic coupling' originated. As a result the first few paragraphs will cover the early history of the articulation before the text goes on to discuss Scammell's place in the medium weight road haulage scene by use of their automatic coupling during the period 1939 to 1980.

The inspiration behind this book was a gift to Venture Publications of a set of photographs and Sales Ledgers from the GSU Company in Manchester courtesy of Mr Saxon Hill, who had been General Manager of that company. GSU were Scammell and Bedford agents and in addition to selling new and used vehicles established one of the earliest and largest trailer hire fleets in the country.

The GSU photographs covered a very interesting period of vehicle design, but were mostly confined to vehicles operating in the North West of England. To compensate for this slightly selective bias, the author has combined the GSU photographs with a selection of photographs from his own collection to give a wider view of the scope of use of the Scammell automatic coupling system within the road haulage industry.

In addition to covering the growth of the Scammell automatic coupling system, the book also details some manufacturers who built trailers and couplings that were more or less compatible with the Scammell system. The book also covers some work of a gifted Scottish vehicle engineer who was able to adapt the automatic coupling system to rigid vehicles!

The modernised design of Karrier Cob featured a Karrier 4-cylinder petrol engine, as opposed to the Jowett 2-cylinder engine fitted in the earliest Cob tractor units. This later model also featured a much improved cab. These Cobs, photographed at the LNER's King's Cross goods depot in 1936, were all fitted with the Scammell compatible 'J' type automatic coupling.

A line-up of Karrier Cob Junior 3-ton capacity tractor units prior to delivery to the LMS Railway, photographed at the Luton factory where production of Karrier models had moved from Huddersfield after the take-over of Karrier Motors by the Rootes Group. Photographs of further developments of Karrier tractor units appear later in the book.

Acknowledgements

Mention must be made at this early stage of friends and colleagues who have helped in the preparation of this book. First and foremost must be Geoff Arnold who came up with the plan for a club for enthusiasts interested in Scammell Mechanical Horses which were fitted with Scammell automatic couplings; secondly Ken Millet of the Mechanical Horse Club whose research into the development of the Mechanical Horse helped considerably in the contents of the book. Mr Saxon Hill of GSU and his son David gave valuable information on the early days of the GSU operation.

A great deal of additional help in getting this book off the ground has been given freely by members of the Mechanical Horse Club, including: Paul Bourne, Paul Cooper, John Downes, Brian Madeley, Sean Madeley, Peter Newman, David Smith and the late David Wood amongst many others. Most of the information on the introduction of the Karrier models came from Ken Millet and I am very grateful for his help on this particular matter. The details of the Australian operation came from David Farrell via Denis Brooks and made very interesting reading. Further details came from Alan Barnes and Gavin Black.

Robin Hannay made an excellent job of reading through the text, adding appropriate comments and correcting the author's errors, for which the author is very grateful.

The author apologises, in advance, if any mistakes are found in the text and would be grateful if the publisher could be contacted to correct the situation. The photographs come from the archive of Venture Publications, GSU and the author's own collection. If any photographs have not been credited to the correct photographer, then please accept our apologies.

In many ways, though, the most important contributor has been the founder of the Mechanical Horse Club, Geoff Arnold. His action in forming the Club resulted in more people being made aware of these vehicles which in turn led to the rescue and preservation of many automatic coupling tractors and trailers which might otherwise have been lost. Without his help this book, and indeed the vehicle preservation scene, would have been much poorer.

Prelude

Firstly, we need to explain the use of the words articulation and automatic coupling. The term 'automatic coupling' was coined later to describe the situation where tractor and trailer could be coupled and uncoupled safely and quickly with no need for the driver to leave the cab of the tractor unit.

Although the concept of articulation had been recognised before the end of the nineteenth century it was never accepted by the early road haulage industry and it was not until the nineteen thirties that the overall concept started to gain favour. Curiously enough, the earliest comprehensive users of the concept were road transports' greatest rivals, the railway companies. Road hauliers eventually realised some of the advantages of articulation using automatic couplings, such as the simple exchange of trailers and the ability of one trailer to be loaded whilst a second was out on delivery with both trailers being handled by one tractor unit. With this realisation then a more comprehensive move towards articulation commenced.

The first recorded British load-carrying articulated unit was a three-wheeled steam tractor built in London by a company called Perkins and Sons in the early 1870s. (Incidentally, the first articulated vehicle was probably a steam coach built by Sir Goldsworth Gurney in 1830.) In Paris, De Dion Bouton produced a form of load-carrying articulated tractor in 1894. Perhaps the most publicised early British articulated combination was a Thornycroft design of 1898 comprising of a steam tractor and 5-ton capacity trailer, relying on a very basic semi-permanent link between tractor and trailer. It would appear that none of the earlier commercial vehicle manufacturers considered that articulation had much of a future since the four-wheeled load-carrying vehicle was to become the most common form of mechanised load carrier in the first 20 years of the 20th Century.

It is perhaps pertinent to recall some of the early legislation with regard to self-propelled road vehicles which certainly retarded the development of road vehicles.

In the late 19th Century, there was a great deal of pro-railway fervour that led to punitive legislation against any form of mechanically-propelled road vehicle. Politicians argued that the railways were the place for machines and the roads should be reserved for horses.

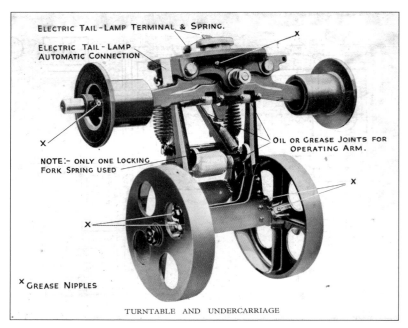

ELECTRIC TAIL-LAMP TERMINAL & SPRING.

ELECTRIC TAIL-LAMP
AUTOMATIC CONNECTION

OIL OR GREASE JOINTS FOR
OPERATING ARM.

NOTE:- ONLY ONE LOCKING
FORK SPRING USED

X GREASE NIPPLES

TURNTABLE AND UNDERCARRIAGE

COUPLING HOOK
AUTOMATIC TAIL-LAMP CONNECTOR
SPRING BUFFER

TRIP GEAR
BACK AXLE FILLER
(FILL TO LEVEL)

Although the Karrier company were the first manufacturer to market a small articulated tractor unit to meet the requirements of the railway companies, the most successful mechanical horse came from the Watford stable of Scammell Lorries. The most important feature of the Scammell horse was the fully automatic coupling designed by Mr OD North and shown here in it's earliest 3-ton form with just one pair of coupling hooks, later altered to two pairs. The most interesting item is the 'trip gear'', a steel tongue which engaged with the roller on the trailer undercarriage to 'fold' the trailer landing frame and wheels up and out of harm's way.

The rear view of the trailer undercarriage clearly shows the flanged wheels that ran up the steel ramps on the tractor unit .

The Locomotives Act of 1861 made it mandatory for any mechanically-propelled vehicle to be preceded by a man with a red flag; there were speed limits of 2mph in towns and 4mph in the country. A further Act of 1865 made it illegal to operate any heavy self-propelled vehicle between the hours of midnight and 6am on Turnpike Roads and made infringements of bridge restrictions liable to heavy penalties; this contrasted greatly with the *laissez-faire* attitude to railway legislation. In 1867 an amendment to the act prohibited the use of an agricultural engine whether stationary, portable or powered within 25 yards of a public roadway.

Thus, the era of horse-drawn portable steam engines began as a way round the Acts. A total of 15 Acts of Parliament were passed between 1860 and 1895, but the wealthy farmers were complaining that these Acts reduced their ability to harvest crops which were required to feed the growing population during the latter part of the industrial revolution. In 1878 the 'Red Flag' requirement was removed, along with some of the restrictions on working hours, (but only for agricultural usage).

It was not until the motor car came on the scene from the 1890s that legislation was gradually reduced. An Act of 1894 removed the 25 yard condition and the Highways Act of 1896 allowed machines of under 3-tons weight (so-called Light Locomotives) to travel up to 12mph.

Because of the restrictions on the use of locomotives, the development of road-going, load-carrying, steam wagons had been seriously retarded and the first load carriers were simply trailer-towing versions of agricultural locomotives.

Quite unusually, the Heavy Motor Car Order of 1904 gave the road vehicle builders almost all the freedom they required at the time. It established overall weights, wheel sizes, brakes, registration marks, lighting and suspension. A heavy motor car was permitted to weigh up to 5-tons unladen; 8-tons was the maximum that could be carried on one axle and gross weight was 12-tons on the whole wagon, with 8-tons allowed on a trailer. The speed limits were complicated, but solo wagons could run at 8mph; if a trailer was towed then the limit was 5mph and if rubber tyres were fitted then the speed could be 12mph if no axle exceeded 6-tons.

Steam wagons were given an additional fillip

from 1908 when the Chancellor of the Exchequer proposed a tax on petrol, but not on coal. These notes show how Parliament expected the railways to carry the majority of goods across the country, a situation which has been turned on its head during the last 100 years.

It was not until 1909 that the concept of a suitable coupling for an articulated vehicle was made available by Charles Martin whose designs were put into production by the Knox Automobile Company in Springfield, Massachusetts. This rapidly led to the introduction of 7 and 12-ton capacity payload tractor/semi-trailer articulated units fitted with the Knox-Martin Rocking Fifth Wheel. The original Knox tractor units were a fairly basic design of bonneted tractor with three-wheel layout, but were soon replaced by a more stable four-wheel version. Although the coupling arrangement did not enable the trailer and tractor to be uncoupled easily, Knox units were used during the First World War and at least one unit entered service with the Great Western Railway and others with Pickfords in the United Kingdom. Very similar versions of this articulated design were produced by AEC and Scammell in the early 1920s, the Scammell design certainly having the fifth wheel mounted directly onto the rear axle of the tractor.

All these very earliest articulated units were virtually permanently coupled combinations, uncoupling the trailer from the tractor was a laborious business involving the placing of separate stands under the trailer for support when uncoupled from the tractor unit.

Across in Germany in the period 1912-1914, the Hansa Company had introduced an articulated coupling arrangement that was semi-automatic, seemingly with a folding landing leg for the trailer complete with a skate type coupling mounted under a turntable that slid onto the tractor chassis. The trailer undercarriage was narrow and appeared to fit between the tractor chassis. However, the most significant point about the tractor and trailer was that it apparently offered a fully-automatic coupling arrangement and the trailer wheels were fully-braked with controls in the cab. Unfortunately, only press advertisements remain to remind historians of this pioneering vehicle design.

The next recorded complete articulated outfit was produced by Lacre's in Letchworth in 1918 and

Although the Karrier Company had built the first successful three-wheel tractor unit for the railway companies, an alternative model was built by the Napier Company at the request of the LNE Railway. One or two prototypes were built before the project was passed to Scammell Lorries and this photograph depicts one of the Napier units with the original style of trailer coupling, but painted in LMS Railway colours.

This photograph shows the ability of the Mechanical Horse to couple with a trailer at a 90 degree angle. The vehicle is probably one of the initial batch of 80 3-ton capacity Mechanical Horses ordered by the London & North Eastern Railway Company.

One of the early three ton capacity Scammell Horses was used as a demonstration unit for this 'Heath Robinson'-style articulated gully emptier built by the Fowler Company of Leeds. The horse is depicted here with the vertical windscreen and deep cowl normally specified by the railway companies. However, the earlier railway horses were not fitted with doors, to save on initial costs, their vehicles being fitted with a simple canvas sheet!

Ordered by the Bognor Regis UDC, this early 3-ton Mechanical Horse displays the hand-operated hydraulic pump used to tip the trailer (two long handles were attached to the short levers protruding from the hydraulic fluid container on the trailer nose). The horse's cab is known as the 'Municipal Type', with a deeper cab than usual to allow the passenger seat to be mounted slightly behind the engine to enable the passenger to rest his feet on the floor. On the standard Mechanical Horse, the only place a passenger could steady himself was on the very hot radiator header tank which was exposed within the cab.

consisted of a standard haulage vehicle combined with a small trailer, and is recorded as having some form of ramp at the rear of the tractor to allow the trailer to couple to the tractor. Unfortunately, this model does not seem to have received any commercial success. No doubt it would have been very expensive when compared with the thousands of ex-military vehicles appearing on the second-hand market at the same time.

In Belgium, Auto-Traction were apparently more successful with their 'Auto Traction Heavy Tractor'. This comprised a four-wheel tractor and semi-trailer with a large, heavy duty, coupling gear, the design of which had possibly originated with Chenard Walcker. The tractor was fitted with a Minerva 60hp petrol engine, 5-speed gearbox and epicyclic final drive, complete with differential lock. Auto-Traction Company was taken over by the Minerva Company in 1925. In the previous year this model was made available in the United Kingdom and was advertised as capable of carrying a 10 ton payload. However, the most significant point about the tractor and trailer was that it offered fully automatic coupling arrangement and the trailer wheels were fully braked. The trailer undercarriage was narrow and appeared to fit between the tractor chassis. Unfortunately again, only press advertisements remain to remind historians of this pioneering vehicle design. It is quite feasible that this model and the earlier Hansa design served as the inspiration for the later coupling arrangements built by the LMS Railway, Karrier Motors and Scammell Lorries.

There is one final early articulated tractor to mention in this prelude to the introduction of the eventual Scammell automatic coupling and this was a fascinating American-designed single axle tractor! It was produced to meet the need to motorise existing horse-drawn vehicles. Named the 'Autohorse' and built by the One Wheel Truck Company of St Louis, Missouri. Powered by a Continental petrol engine of 22hp it had a 3-speed gearbox and a gear drive to the single front wheel. It was designed to clamp to the front axle of the horse vehicle, but had retractable wheels for solo running. This amazing vehicle was first produced in 1917 and one came to Britain in 1922 and it was trialed by the London Midland and Scottish Railway, but was considered unsuitable for further development.

Reverting to the adoption of articulation within the United Kingdom, as mentioned above, it was a very similar concept to the American Knox articulated vehicle that G Scammell and Nephew of Spitalfields in East London adopted for their famous 'articulated six-wheeler' of 1919. This company was initially based on the coach-building skills of George Scammell and his company who had become an agent for Foden steam wagons and the petrol powered commercial vehicles known as Commer Cars. The nephew in the company title was Richard Scammell.

Other members of the Scammell family worked in the business including Alfred George Scammell, who was a Lieutenant Colonel during the First World War. He returned from war service convinced that he could produce a far more efficient load carrying vehicle than those currently available. Whether he had seen or heard of the Knox unit is debatable, but he certainly appreciated the payload bonus that articulation gave over rigid vehicles. Here, the advantage of articulation was not necessarily the easily detachable trailer, but the additional payload available at nominal extra cost. Hence, in the advertising blurb of the time '7½ tons carrying capacity at 3-tons cost and speed'. Almost as important was the fact that the taxation on this type of vehicle was lower than the tax for the equivalent rigid six-wheel lorry. This issue of taxation was based on the fact that the new Ministry of Transport decided that any articulated outfits could be classed as single units rather than a tractor and trailer combination.

There was a restriction placed on this new idea in that axle loading for the third axle must not exceed 6-tons and as long as the unladen weight of this articulated unit did not exceed 5-tons it could travel at a maximum speed of 12mph. Quite amazingly, under those same regulations the articulated combination was also able to tow a separate small trailer giving a payload potential of 13½ tons, compared with perhaps 6-tons on a four-wheel vehicle.

The first Scammell articulated units built from 1919 utilised an almost identical coupling to that fitted to the Knox tractors with a turntable plate mounted directly onto the rear axle via an individual pair of leaf springs. A separate lighter section chassis carried the engine and gearbox along with the cab and front wheels, this chassis having its own pair of rear leaf springs The king-

Just to prove that recycling' is nothing new, Phillips Mills of Battersea, London were collecting paper and card for re-use before World War II with this 6-ton capacity Mechanical Horse.

A quite atmospheric shot of an early 3-ton Mechanical Horse in use with the LNER, probably at Nottingham, loading some hogsheads containing tobacco leaf to be used at one of the local cigarette factories.

pin for these units was fitted directly onto the tractor rubbing plate and since there were no such luxuries as lead-on ramps and guides, the coupling of tractor and trailer was not a job to be lightly undertaken.

In view of the potential business generated by the new Scammell six-wheeler, and with expansion restricted at the Spitalfields site, a new works was established by Scammell Lorries at Watford. The original London company continued in business as coachbuilders. Very soon the Watford factory, under the control of Lt Col Alfred George Scammell, with help from his brother James Allen Scammell, was producing a wide range of heavy duty articulated tractors and trailers, including bulk tankers, low-load trailers as well as platform trailers.

Of course, every successful concept has its imitators and other lorry manufacturers soon offered models suitable for conversion to articulated tractors, albeit in very small quantities. By the late 1920s articulated units were an established concept, mostly as heavy duty vehicles designed to carry heavy or abnormal loads over long distances and often used for bulk liquid haulage, but interestingly there were very few contemporaneous small articulated vehicles. In fact, the world in general and the medium size vehicle user in particular were well catered for by the smaller rigid petrol-engined van or commercial or indeed by the horse and cart.

Although the Scammell Mechanical Horse was designed as an articulated tractor, it was occasionally used as a rigid vehicle. The most common version was used as a small dustcart with a 'Chelsea' or chip pan style body, but Benskin's Brewery of Watford bought one for local bottled beer distribution. These rigid MHs had a specially manufactured straight chassis frame and were fitted with the 6-ton rear axle with larger section wheels and tyres.

The Railway's Influence

There was, however, one group of companies within the United Kingdom that were quite forward thinking as far as new concepts in land transport were concerned. The group members were the nominally independent regional railway companies that had been formed in 1923. The main constituents comprised the Great Western, the Southern, London, Midland & Scottish and the London & North Eastern Railways. As strange as it may seem these days the railway companies were the only operators to offer a fully nationwide goods collection and delivery service for all manner of goods from a needle to an industrial transformer or an eel to an elephant across the length and breadth of the United Kingdom. As major goods services providers the railway companies introduced many new ancillary road collection and delivery services based purely on the use of mechanically-driven vehicles that were well beyond the capabilities of the horse and wagon. These new services were introduced to encourage more potentially profitable traffic onto the railway network.

The companies operated a large number of small vans for the express parcel deliveries alongside an extensive fleet of 2 and 4-ton lorries and vans that was utilised both for the movement of heavier items and on the rural delivery routes. These vehicles worked from about 4,700 stations and depots and made use of around 18,000 horses with about 30,000 of their attendant load-carrying drays. The railway companies' problem lay in finding a suitable replacement to take the place of the horse on town deliveries and collections; an operation generally described as 'town cartage'. On this work the basic manoeuvrability of the horse and dray in the extremely restricted railway depots and also in the very crowded towns with their poor access for deliveries into shop and factory premises made it almost irreplaceable. Because of the comprehensive network of railway routes with depots spread right across the country there were few long distance road delivery routes. The collection and delivery network was simply a multitude of many short journeys to and from the depots. This was the type of work ideally suited to the horse and dray, with the empty and full drays being exchanged at the depots perhaps three and four times within a shift with the horse

With the acceptance of the Mechanical Horse concept into local authority use, a number were purchased by Westminster Council in London. However, some of them were converted when new to battery-electric traction including this one by Electricar. The idea was that with 24-hour operation of services, the silent operation of this model would not disturb the residents. However, it is quite likely that the exhauster used to create a vacuum in the gully emptier tank would be far noisier than a petrol engine!

simply transferring between returning empty and pre-loaded drays ready for delivery. The railway companies realised that this operation was crying out to be mechanised yet the only vehicles available from the existing manufacturers were either fairly lightweight or, at the other end of the scale, medium to heavy duty sturdily built load carriers. None of these vehicles offered the required manoeuvrability nor any suitable means of quickly and simply exchanging empty and loaded drays and this made the search for replacements for the horse fraught with difficulties.

Undaunted by this singular lack of appropriate equipment the London Midland & Scottish Railway decided (with the agreement of the other railway companies) to experiment with a variety of different motive units to replace the horse. Suffice to say that the ultimate proposal was a three-wheeled petrol engined unit with a coupling designed by the LMS engineers.

KARRIER

'BANTAM' 4-5 TON TRACTOR

PETROL OR DIESEL   A ROOTES PRODUCT

By the mid-thirties Scammell Lorries had successfully built a large number of 'frameless' tankers. These tanks made use of the inherent strength of the tank shell to replace the conventional chassis on the trailer and all running gear and coupling equipment was mounted directly on the tank. This particular horse was supplied to the Imperial Chemical Industries subsidiary in Oldbury who traded as Chance and Hunt. The tank was most likely glass or rubber lined to prevent corrosion to the steel barrel and was provided with rubber pockets (or bibs) to collect any chemical spillage when being loaded.

Karrier Motors Input

In 1929 Karrier Motors Ltd of Huddersfield had introduced their Karrier Colt petrol-engined three-wheeled load carrier. This vehicle was designed in recognition of the need for a small capacity, highly manoeuvrable refuse vehicle that could operate in the alleyways, courtyards and narrow streets in the older parts of towns and cities.

This small vehicle, powered by a Jowett air-cooled two-stroke petrol engine and fitted with solid tyres, came to the attention of the LMS engineers in 1929 and one chassis and cab was supplied to the LMS Railway. At the time the railway company had an enormous stock of existing horse-drawn drays and it was the intention that the new tractor unit, based on the Karrier chassis, could couple to those drays. The original design of the tractor coupling enabled the dray's front axle to be lifted hydraulically (hand pumped) over the tractor's rear axle. This new tractor unit became known, quite appropriately as the Karrier Cob.

The GWR and LNER acquired prototype Karrier Cob tractors for experimental purposes, but towards the end of 1930 it became clear that the use of unmodified horse drays was unsatisfactory. Coupling of the two components, (tractor and dray) was cumbersome and braking arrangements for the trailer, where they existed, were primitive. The LMS reverted to a design of coupling which took the form of a pair of inverted channel section steel ramps on the tractor unit with small rollers mounted under the trailer's turntable. The rollers ran up the ramps and the trailer turntable had a small pair of steel road wheels mounted on fixed legs at the extreme edge of the trailer for use when the trailer was uncoupled. The prototype coupling was designed and built at the LMS Road Vehicle workshops in Buckinghamshire and henceforward was known as the 'Wolverton Coupling'.

The LNER then decided on a different approach, which was to lead to the eventual breakthrough in automatic coupling. This breakthrough initially involved Karrier Motors who were requested to update the earlier Cob model by providing a more powerful engine, a compatible, and purpose-built, semi-trailer with brakes operated from the driving position and a fully-automatic coupling arrangement. Karrier were told that substantial orders would follow from a successful trial.

Thomas Bantock & Company of Wolverhampton were Goods Agents for the Great Western Railway and undertook goods deliveries and collections within the Wolverhampton area. Quite unusually they were able to advertise their allegiance to the railway company whilst retaining their own vehicle livery. This photograph was taken on Tolpits Lane, outside the Scammell factory and shows the local allotments with their chestnut paling fences and, behind, the chimney of the Watford Steam Laundry.

During the late 1930s a number of Bedford W Series short wheelbase chassis were converted into 6-ton capacity tractor units by the addition of an articulated coupling gear, plus possible alterations to rear springs, rear axle ratios and braking system modifications. One such unit is seen here in use with the Grand Union Canal Company and had been fitted with Scammell 6-ton automatic coupling gear.

It is possible that the first fleet of non-Scammell built tractor units (ie not Mechanical Horses) to be fitted with Scammell automatic couplings belonged to the LMS Railway, who ordered a batch of Dennis 40/45cwt chassis in 1938 for modifying into tractor units. Here, one is seen coupled to a 'glass float' trailer, capable of safely transporting sheets of glass or marble or other fragile, but difficult to handle products. *(A Ingram)*

The Great Western Railway decided to use some Thornycroft Nippy 3-ton chassis as a base for their 6-ton capacity automatic coupling tractors. This late 1938 Nippy is fitted with a GWR-designed 'Safety Cab' rather than one built to the manufacturers` standard design. The sliding cab door in theory allowed the driver to get into and out of the cab more easily and also enabled the driver to look out and reverse in relative safety.

Occasionally, the Scammell factory management would allow the vehicle manufacturers to fit the automatic coupling gear onto tractor chassis at the manufacturers` works. This is happening here with Thornycroft Nippy chassis having the coupling gear mounted at Thornycroft's Basingstoke factory, probably during the 1938-39 period and destined for the Great Western Railway company.

Within three months Karrier had satisfied the LNER requirements and the production version of the new tractor, designated the Cob Major, made its debut in mid-1931. The Karrier coupling design was very similar in operation to the Wolverton style of coupling, though probably not compatible. The Karrier coupling became known as the AK and later as the slightly modified BK model which Karrier continued to offer through to the 1950s. This coupling was incompatible with the later Scammell coupling and featured trailer landing wheels fitted outside the tractor unit's rear wheels, as shown in the photograph at the top of page 25.

The Cob Major tractor was fitted with a Coventry Climax 4-cylinder petrol engine complete with slightly more modern and definitely larger cab whilst the chassis had pneumatic tyres and in 1934 the design was further updated with a Karrier 27hp engine and further improved cab, the unit and trailer being capable of carrying 4-ton loads. The following year Karrier Motors were absorbed into the Rootes Group and in 1936 a fully revised Cob Major built at the Luton factory entered production.

The new model, fitted with a Rootes petrol engine, competed with the newly introduced 4-wheel Karrier Bantam tractor. There was a Karrier Cob Senior model, capable of handling 6-ton loads, but unlike its Scammell counterpart it was not designed to cope with overloads, so in hilly areas the load would need to be reduced. (It has been stated elsewhere that Scammell's would always base their vehicles carrying capacity on what the vehicle could cope with on a steep hill, whilst their competitors would use a flat road for comparison!) A Karrier Cob Junior was also built at Luton, this smaller model catered for 3-ton loads. The Cob range remained available until 1939 when Rootes were forced to concentrate on military production for the war effort. Post-war the four-wheel Karrier Bantam became the smallest Rootes commercial. Although a revamped Cob tractor prototype was built soon after the war, full production was never commenced, leaving the three-wheel market open to the competitors.

The first Bedford/Scammell combinations sold jointly between Bedford and Scammell were based on the 'W' series chassis, but in 1939 the 'O' Series Bedford was announced. However, before serious production could commence, the Second World War started and the Bedford factory manufactured a slightly different version of the 'O' Series with a squarer bonnet assembly known as the 'OXC'. Many thousands were built for the war effort, including this unit complete with frameless tank for transporting fuel.

A Major Re-development

Although the Karrier Cob became the first direct replacement for the flesh horse, an upstart whose origins go back to early 1931 soon surpassed it. In that year the London & North Eastern Railway decided to sponsor an alternative vehicle to the Karrier offered from Huddersfield. Although the LNER had already purchased a number of Karrier Cobs in 1931, it appears that financial problems at Karrier Motors Ltd had forced them to reduce the range of vehicles currently in production and production of the Cob was temporarily phased out. The LNER did not wish to develop a horse replacement vehicle by themselves, but did establish the basic specification for such a beast as noted above. An agent was then engaged to find a manufacturer willing to undertake the necessary development. The agent met by chance an engineer from the D Napier & Sons Company who themselves were looking for work as a result of both the general economic depression and the fact that no re-armament was being considered in Britain at the time. The outcome of the meeting was that Napier agreed to develop a three-wheeled tractor. The company

built a prototype that met with LNER approval, but then Napier's decided not to proceed with the project. The agent then approached Scammell Lorries who agreed to take over the work. All of the Napier prototypes, manufacturing rights and tooling were passed to Scammell's at Watford.

At that time the Chief Designer at Scammell's was Mr OD North, a very lateral thinker who had already designed the Auto Van, the North Lucas car, whilst plans for the 6-wheel Scammell Pioneer were on the drawing board. He acknowledged the innovative nature of the Napier design, but felt that certain fundamental changes would enhance the commercial viability of the vehicle. The original Napier design of coupling gear had close similarities to the LMS Wolverton coupling, complete with external trailer jockey wheels and was in desperate need of redesign. It was up to Mr North to 'pull a rabbit out of a hat' and this he did with consummate style. Even though his design was slightly reminiscent of the earlier Minerva automatic coupling, there were many advanced features to make the Scammell coupling unique.

The railway company had specified the need for the coupling to work with loaded or empty trailers, to work on any road surface (generally

The British Insulated Callendar's Cables Company had factories in Lancashire where they used a wide variety of Scammell equipment, including this immediate post-war 3/6-ton Mechanical Horse. This unusual designation meant it was a 3-ton horse, but with strengthened chassis to cope with 6-ton loads.

the setts or cobbles to be found in railway yards), at any reasonable angle between tractor and trailer and to be the ultimate in simplicity. In fact they wanted the coupling to work automatically!

The coupling to suit these criteria was designed by Mr North, and was in concept quite simple, though very ingenious in design and engineering terms, and this was fitted to a Scammell-modified, Napier three-wheeled chassis.

On the Scammell redesign of the original Napier Mechanical Horse the rear chassis cross-member was omitted completely and two narrow, rather bent looking, pressed steel channel section ramps were mounted on the appropriately shaped rear chassis frames. The front of the ramps were joined by a massive box section cross-member on which was mounted the locking device. On the early trailers this lock was a pair of claws, but was soon modified to incorporate two pairs of claws that engaged with two pairs of small rollers that were mounted on the underside of the trailer's turntable. Fitted to the front of the ramp were spring-loaded buffers and 'C' shaped retaining hooks to prevent lateral and vertical movement of the trailer when coupled. The job of the buffers was to 'load' the coupling hooks to ensure that the trailer was securely locked to the unit. On the trailer itself the coupling components consisted of a forged beam that pivoted on the turntable, this enabled the trailer chassis to move in relation to the unit. At the end of this beam were two flanged steel wheels. Under the forged beam were a series of paired, hinged metal struts that made up the undercarriage and this ran on two large steel jockey wheels.

The crowning glory of the Scammell design was that, unlike any of the earlier designs, the whole coupling process was fully automatic. To couple the unit and trailer together all the driver had to do was to reverse his Mechanical Horse towards the trailer. As the driver reversed the small flanged wheels travelled up the ramp lifting the jockey wheels off the ground. As the driver reversed even further a spring loaded catch forced the undercarriage to fold up (or retract) backwards thereby giving increased ground clearance. Simultaneously, the claws on the tractor engaged with the rollers mounted under the forged beam giving a positive connection.

The trailer's brakes were mechanically operated by a centrally mounted slipper pad on the

tractor's coupling gear making direct contact with various bell cranks and levers operating through the central turntable and then a rod linkage to the rear axle of the trailer. The lighting connection consisted of direct contact between two brass plates mounted on both parts of the combination. The braking system was so arranged that the trailer brakes should operate fractionally before the unit's brakes to help the whole combination stop in a straight line. As far as the driver was concerned he had only to release the trailer's mechanical handbrake and move the registration plate and rear light (lights from the 1950s) to the rear of the trailer from the tractor unit. (At that time there was no legal requirement for the tractor unit to have rear lights when coupled to a trailer with lights). The driver had no need to line up the tractor and trailer accurately since the coupling gear took care of that. Unlike current articulated units there were no landing legs for the driver to wind up (or down), no electrical and air or vacuum brake hoses to connect between tractor and trailer. This new coupling was able to meet all the criteria set out by the LMS Railway back in 1929 in that it would couple at any angle, on any surface and in laden or unladen condition.

The tractor unit was also substantially modified from the original Napier design. It was already much larger than the original Karrier Cob and featured a water-cooled 10hp 4-cylinder petrol engine. The Scammell Company had envisaged three payload capacities of tractor unit, three, five and six tons, but when full production commenced the 5-ton version was quickly dropped. The new vehicle was called the 'Mechanical Horse', because that is exactly what it was. The new 'horse' was shown to the public for the first time in late 1932 and was in full production the following year. Like its Yorkshire sister, the 'horse' could turn on a sixpence due to its single front wheel, and with trailer attached had a turning circle of less than 18ft. The success of the design led to an immediate order from the LNER for 80 tractors and 113 trailers. Once the LMS Railway accepted the simple and foolproof nature of the automatic coupling they virtually ceased production of their own Wolverton coupling and bought complete units from the Watford works of Scammell Lorries.

Mr North understandably had reservations about the ability of the 3-ton size of coupling to accept 6-

The operation of buses and coaches in London was carried out by London Transport, who also used a fleet of lorries to supply the bus fleet. As well as looking after the passenger carrying vehicles, London Transport purchased a small number of mobile canteens to refresh driving and platform staff at terminal locations where there were no existing catering facilities. Here is one of the 10 units supplied between 1947 and 1949.

A photograph to send shudders down the spine of readers of a certain age? Some 1,500 gallons of Cod Liver Oil could be carried in the Bedford/Scammell elliptical frameless tanker combination, belonging to the British Cod Liver Oil Company of Hull. The small tube fitted to the offside of the trailer carries the flexible hoses used for delivery purposes.

In the period between the end of the Second World War and nationalisation of the railways in 1948, the Rootes Group brought out a fully updated version of the pre-war Karrier Cob tractor unit. A prototype was photographed at the LNER Luton Hoo station, complete with an LMS trailer. Unfortunately, no orders for this new model seem to have been placed, instead the four-wheeled Karrier Bantam tractor unit was ordered. *(P Newman)*

Prior to the placing of bulk orders for new vehicles the railway companies would often test the one vehicle, as seen here in North Yorkshire with a nearly new wooden cabbed Karrier Bantam thought to be on test near Sutton Bank. *(Courtesy HS Transport Collection)*

The Karrier Bantam four-wheel chassis was introduced in the mid-thirties as a small load carrier. It was soon made available as a tractor unit to supplement the three-wheel Cob models, albeit at a slight loss of ultimate manoeuvrability. The majority of Bantams were sold with the Scammell compatible 'J' type coupling, but Karrier also offered their own 'BK' articulated coupling as seen here with an East Midlands Gas Board tractor unit, the trailer being fitted with the wide spaced landing wheels. *(Courtesy A Ingram)*

Owned by the City of Westminster, this Karrier Bantam is fitted with Karrier's own Scammell-compatible 'J' type coupling and is seen here street washing in London's Piccadilly, with a two-man crew, the trailer man working the tank discharge valves.

ton loads and designed a slightly larger, but totally incompatible coupling for 6-ton loads. This was fitted to the 6-ton Mechanical Horse, which differed from its smaller brother by having larger rear wheels and a 15hp 4-cylinder petrol engine.

In fact, the whole concept was so sound that although Karrier had been the real originator of the idea, they very soon had to offer their own version of the Scammell 3-ton coupling known as the 'J' type to ensure that they would still receive orders for new vehicles from the railway companies with a coupling that was compatible with the Scammell-built trailers. In order to get round the Scammell patents the coupling differed from the Scammell design by using positively sprung 'C' shaped hooks which fitted over the small flanged wheels so as to retain the trailer coupling in position rather than the central hooks of the Scammell version.

One of the first pre-production prototypes of the Scammell Mechanical Horse was exhibited at the Scottish Motor Show late in 1932 and on 3rd June 1933 the trade newspaper *Motor Transport* devoted a whole page article to the new horses and noted that many modifications had been made to the vehicles in the months since the Scottish Show. On demonstration at Kings Langley near Watford, the *Motor Transport* journalist found that a loaded 3-ton horse could climb a steady gradient of 1 in 7½. It could stop and start easily on the same gradient and also turn round on the same hill, which was 18ft wide, and would also couple and uncouple on the same gradient. Though built to the same basic design as the Karrier Cob it was a little more sophisticated than its competitor. Once the trade had been made aware of the new vehicle it was finally presented to an unsuspecting public on 7th September 1933.

Interestingly, none of the European designs appear to have been taken up by British manufacturers and by 1938 versions of the Scammell coupling were being manufactured in France by the FAR Company. The only likely contender to the Scammell system appeared to be the Auto-Retractor system manufactured by Carrimore, but was never to achieve the success of Scammell's unit.

Once the basic design of three-wheeler tractor and its attendant trailers was settled, and production was under way for railway companies, both Scammell and the Rootes

Group set about widening the market for this unique concept. The main marketing ploy hinged around the ultimate versatility of the vehicles; for not only could they replace the four legged horse and not need carefully looking after 365 days per year, they could also give major increases in productivity. A single Mechanical Horse or Cob Major could carry up to a 6-ton payload. Whilst one trailer was being loaded another trailer could be out on delivery and a third could be discharging its load – and all these trailers could be handled by a single tractor unit. In addition a wide variety of alternative trailer bodies or styles were made available. The main question was, whom should the salesman direct his effort towards? At the time of the Mechanical Horses' introduction the whole country was attempting to drag itself out of the early 1930s depression and there was not a great deal of money about. However, certain markets could afford to purchase new vehicles especially if these new vehicles could offer real value for money in increased productivity.

Who were these potential customers? Well, of course, the brewers, gas manufacturing companies, electricity companies, municipal authorities, dairies, coal merchants and retailing chains all of whom could be described as relatively wealthy with guaranteed markets. What all these operators had in common were urban operations, often with protracted loading times and with a need to replace flesh horses and exchange trailers on a very regular basis.

Scammell's publicity stated that by 1939 over 60 municipalities alone had 'revolutionised' (Scammell's words) their transport with the introduction of Scammell-based cleansing vehicles including street washers, gully emptiers, bin carriers and refuse collectors.

Generally speaking, the sale of one tractor could usually guarantee the sale of at least two trailers (or carriers as Scammell quaintly called them).

A little later substantial numbers of Mechanical Horses entered Government service mainly with the Army and RAF. Their main use was in Ordnance and repair depots where their ultimate manoeuvrability in confined spaces was valuable. It is thought that some were used by the naval authorities on aircraft carriers to move planes around below decks.

Driver C Chadburn of Burton on Trent BR (LM) Region goods depot smiles having accepted First Prize for the best maintained vehicle, in this case a 3-ton Scammell Mechanical Horse alongside an Austin K2 and a Karrier Bantam sporting the wooden cab that was used on the four-wheel Bantam that generally superseded the three-wheel Karrier Cob tractor unit after the war.

The British Broadcasting Corporation used a variety of vehicles in its Outside Broadcasting operation, including this Bedford OSS with van bodied drop frame trailer, possibly a control room and almost certainly full of very expensive equipment.

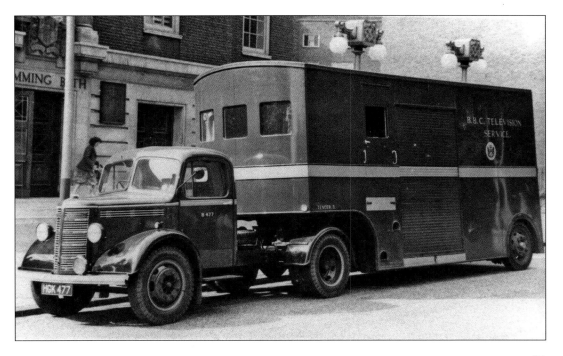

Although designed with local delivery use in mind the 6-ton automatic coupling gear gradually came to the notice of the road hauliers. By converting a rigid vehicle to an articulated combination a useful doubling of payload could be gained for less than the cost of buying two rigid vehicles. During the thirties a number of manufacturers were already offering articulated conversions to new four-wheeled short wheelbase haulage chassis, using a very basic coupling. Many of the earlier conversions featured various Bedford models due to their inherent inbuilt capacity to be overloaded.

Of all the articulated converters the name of Carrimore Six Wheelers of Finchley is perhaps best known. Their conversion on Bedford chassis was introduced in 1935. These conversions proved that articulation could be successfully applied to mass-produced trucks as well as to the higher priced and higher quality heavy duty models. Other well-known names involved with early-articulated conversions include:

BTC (The British Trailer Company)

Taskers of Andover

The Truck and Tractor Appliance Co of Trafford
   Park, Manchester
   (whose trailer was called the Dragon)

Eagle of Warwick

Flexicon from Hendon in North London
   and interestingly

G Scammell and Nephew of Spitalfields, London.

These companies were all amongst the leaders in this particular market. The majority of these articulated combinations simply took advantage of the additional payload that could be gained rather than the possibility of using different trailers. The Dragon trailer was featured quite widely in the press releases of the time (mid-'30s) and stated that a Thornycroft truck of 2-ton capacity could legally carry a 3½ ton payload. It also propounded that running costs came to only 1d (½p) per mile and that it took only a minute to uncouple the trailer. Not all these conversions used a fifth wheel as we know them today. Often a simple circular steel frame with a central locating pin was used, certainly few of the manufacturers offerings were standardised.

From the sparse records that are available it appears that it may have been the LMS Railway who brought the concept of Scammell automatic coupling fitted to four-wheelers to fruition. They combined a short wheelbase Dennis 40/45cwt chassis/cab with the 6-ton Scammell MH coupling gear and ordered a batch in early 1938. These Dennis tractors were soon followed by some Thornycroft Nippy 3-ton chassis converted with 6-ton automatic coupling for use on the Great Western Railway. Without a doubt, a number of individual Bedford chassis had been converted to accept Scammell couplings before 1938, but it appears to have been the LMS Railway who placed the first large order for Scammell-converted tractors.

Designed for the town delivery of rapidly diminishing loads, the Ford-engined Jensen Tug was capable of taking 1½ ton loads. This model had a unique style of automatic coupling, totally incompatible with any others in use on the railway network. The coupling consisted of a single run-up ramp and a trailer undercarriage with landing wheels at the extremities, requiring the tractor to be fitted with a narrow-track rear axle.

Photographed in Derby in post-nationalisation livery is one of the many thousands of Mechanical Horses supplied to the railway companies. This is a 3-ton model with vertical windscreen, deep cowl and basic door and shed door catch. Behind the trailer can be seen a remarkable variety of goods that were handled by the railway operation up to the 1960s.

For many years the majority of brewery companies were able to purchase vehicles with high quality bodywork to promote the quality of their beers. This early post war Dennis Horla tractor unit has a basic trailer chassis fitted with three steel barrels finished to look like wood and used by Watney's in London for deliveries to local pubs and clubs.

This driver of this 6-ton capacity Mechanical Horse is seen being directed safely in a reverse manoeuvre by a colleague. The photograph was one of a series taken around St Albans in the early 1950s as part of a safe driving campaign. The horse has been fitted with rubber corners to the cab cowl in order to reduce damage in the close confines of railway goods depots. *(Courtesy C Green)*

The Jensen Company in West Bromwich designed a small mechanical horse for town deliveries of goods. Unfortunately, whilst fitted with a form of automatic coupling, it was totally incompatible with the Scammell version. The capacity of the complete vehicle was 1½ tons and was purchased in small numbers by British Railways, amongst other users. Its small size and use of car derived running units meant it did not easily stand up to the rough and tumble of railway use and in general did not last long in railway service. Despite this Arthur Ingram photographed this 1953 example in North London in the late 1950s. *(Courtesy of A Ingram)*

Far removed from the hustle and bustle of parcels delivery work was this Jensen Jen Tug delivered in 1951 to M Jackson for coal deliveries in the delightful town of Louth in Lincolnshire. *(Courtesy HLH)*

By the mid-1940s the original Scammell Mechanical Horse was showing it's age and in 1948 a brand new model was brought out called the Scammell Scarab. Here is an early view of a possibly pre-production 6-ton Scarab, clearly showing the offset gate change gear lever, centrally placed radiator between the seats, basic steering gear and the three levers: tractor handbrake, trailer handbrake and trailer uncoupling lever. To the uninitiated driver entering the cab for the first time, these levers must have seemed quite intimidating!

Vauxhall Become More Aware

The success of the LMS project must have reached the ears of the management at Vauxhall Motors because they really took the Scammell coupling concept to heart and the market for Scammell automatic couplings was soon to grow.

At the Scottish Motor Show in the autumn of 1938 a matched Bedford-Scammell combination was displayed and they were officially launched on the 3rd February 1939 with models for 6 to 8-ton loads available direct from Bedford dealers.

For 6-ton loads the Bedford WHG nominal 2-ton chassis was utilised while the 8-tonner relied on the heavier duty Bedford WTH 3-ton chassis. The most important item to note about the link between Scammell and Bedford was that the unit and trailer could be ordered as a complete package from the Bedford dealer. The tractor was built to the correct specification to suit the Scammell coupling gear by having a modified chassis frame and rear springs to fit under the Scammell coupling, as well as different rear axle ratios and, of course, uprated brakes. The Bedford dealer could handle any warranty problems on either truck or coupling.

The close working relationship between Bedford and Scammell was in complete contrast to problems that could potentially arise with other coupling and trailer manufacturers with each blaming the other when warranty faults arose. The cost of the Bedford tractor unit was £280 when they were officially announced. One important modification was to the braking system, with all the four-wheel tractor units gaining power operation of the mechanical trailer brakes through a vacuum cylinder mounted on the tractor which operated the slipper which connected to the trailer's foundation brakes.

One big advantage of articulated trailers over drawbar trailers towed by a rigid lorry was that no second man was needed in the cab to work the trailer brakes. Originally, there seemed to be no legal requirement for the trailer brakes to be connected to the tractor unit foundation brakes. This would have been difficult with the non-power assisted cable or rod operated brakes which were prevalent at the time on lorries and meant that it was essential to have a second mate to manually operate the separate cable-operated trailer brakes. Once vacuum brakes came into general use on heavier lorries the trailer brakes could be applied by the driver, but legislation by then still dictated the need for a second man to be in the cab and this situation remained so until 1970 for rigid lorries with drawbar trailers.

Despite the fact that a normal 3/4-ton payload vehicle such as a Bedford W type, Thornycroft Nippy or even a Dennis 40/45cwt chassis could be expected to be overloaded during normal operations, it still seems strange that a basic 3-ton lorry could be converted to haul a payload of 6-tons or more with few alterations to the basic chassis.

Apart from modifying the chassis frame to fit the relatively low mounting of the automatic coupling alternative up-rated rear springs were fitted to the chassis as well. The petrol engines generally would have had enlarged carburettor jets installed to give more power. In most cases the tractor units' brakes would have been altered by Scammell to include servo assistance and generally the rear axle differential would be altered to one with a higher ratio. By no means was the vehicle designed specifically for these heavier duties, the simple conversion was carried out at the lowest cost and certainly these basic conversions could not take place today under EC regulations.

Excess demand for Scammell's lorries and trailers early in the war meant that a shadow factory was set up lower down Tolpits Lane, Watford in 1940 and was known as the Moor Park Works. This plant was extended in 1941 and was later designated as the main trailer works and produced a wide range of trailers for both military use and for allocation to those road hauliers who could prove to the Ministry of War Transport that they had need for one. Production of trailers at the Moor Park works continued into the 1970s.

As mentioned earlier, the Karrier Cob had been updated regularly during its production run up to the outset of the Second World War. In contrast, the Mechanical Horse remained very much as originally built right through from 1932 up to 1948. In fact, the design and build quality was such that it was relatively indestructible. That is not to say it did not have drawbacks; it was slow, the engine still had no self-starter and with the engine mounted high up and offset to the left, the vehicles had a tendency to fall on their side on

Scammell Scarab JNK 914 was one of the more photographed early demonstration 6-ton Scarab tractor units. It is seen here in the British Railways London Midland Region goods depot at Watford Junction, posed for the photographer. However, of even more interest to generations of Watford residents is the Ford van in the background. It belonged to Keens of Watford who were renowned for their pie and sausage-making prowess.

In addition to the 6-ton Mechanical Horses operated by Watneys in London, the company also purchased this 3-ton Scarab complete with short trailer in 1951. No doubt the manoeuvrability of the unit was a great asset in crowded city streets. *(Courtesy K Upson)*

Mortimers Dairies in Sussex bought this 3-ton Scammell Scarab in early 1951 to move crated milk between dairy and depots. Unusually, the trailer is fitted with 10.50x13 wheels and tyres, a combination normally only found on the 6-ton capacity trailers and may have been an ex-military purchase. In the cab can be seen two 'C' licence discs, these were issued by the Ministry of Transport in the days before Operators Licensing, one for the tractor and one for the trailer.

This 1952 Scammell Scarab 6-ton tractor unit was used by British Insulated Callendar's Cables for the collection of coal from local mines in Lancashire as well as collecting and delivering goods from the local railway depot. BICC were a very good customer of GSU. The GSU management recall an incident when a new Scarab was being reversed under a loaded trailer, but driver lost his nerve during the coupling procedure and the heavy trailer simply 'spat' the Scarab out and in doing so managed to reverse the rotation of the engine, which promptly went into 'orbit'! *(Courtesy BICC)*

A view of a Thompson-built elliptical four-compartment road tanker purchased by Shell Mex and BP for fuel or oil deliveries coupled to a Leyland Comet tractor unit. This photograph shows how neatly the trailer undercarriage folded away behind the tractor's rear axle. When new this vehicle was legally subject to a 20mph speed limit. This old fashioned rule was abolished for commercial vehicles in 1955. *(RN Hannay)*

Many of the Midlands-based car manufacturers had factories spread across a wide area. Consequently, road transport was used to move components between sites. The Scammell auto coupling trailers were ideal for this work as the tractor unit could easily exchange full and empty trailers and, in times of production delays, the trailers could act as storage units.

tight right hand turns. A revised model was well overdue by the mid-1940s, but of necessity needed to retain the basic coupling gear design and three wheels of the Mechanical Horse due to the large numbers of existing 3 or 6-ton trailers in use and the essential need for manoeuvrability.

The completely new horse was introduced by Scammell in 1948 with the petrol engine, gearbox and rear axle combined in one unit and mounted low in the chassis offering extra traction on the rear axle. The original style of coupling gear was, of course, retained in 3 and 6-ton versions, though uprated. A brand new steel cab was built by the Willenhall Motor and Radiator Company, using some of the pressings already in use for the Bedford 'O' Series of trucks. The name for the new beast was decided by combining the names of the best breeds of commercial vehicle and horse resulting in the glorious combination of **SCA**mmell and **ARAB** to become the **SCARAB**. In fact, the way these vehicles scurried about in busy yards did remind one of the Egyptian Scarab beetle.

The Scarab tractor unit in both versions was an immediate success; it appealed to the existing users of Mechanical Horses and with its additional power, offered a higher top speed, enabling more work to be carried out in a given time. Drivers found it a relatively more comfortable vehicle and fitters found that the engine was more easily accessible for maintenance. British Railways had been formed in 1948 from the previously nominally independent railway companies and they immediately placed orders for the new model.

The four-wheel Karrier Bantam was itself able to make up lost ground in the fifties and sixties with large sales to British Railways. The Karrier-designed BK coupling of the Cob and Bantam was built in just one size for 3, 4 or potentially 6-ton loads, whilst the Scammell-compatible J type Karrier coupling was designed for the 3-ton coupling fitted to the smaller capacity Scammell trailers. Scammell retained two sizes of coupling gear, one for 3-ton and a larger version for 6-ton loads. The Karrier Bantam was built with a wood-framed cab up till 1951 when a slightly modified version of the Rootes Group all-steel Commer cab became available.

Victor Value were a North London-based supermarket chain operating at the less expensive end of the market and were taken over by Tesco in 1968. Their transport operation was partly based around the use of Scammell automatic coupling vehicles as typified by this Bedford SA unit. The hydraulic ram interposed between tractor and trailer was supplied by Adrolic. The idea was that hydraulic damping in the device would reduce the potential for a jackknife under extreme braking conditions.

Heavier Models

Reverting to the heavier duty models, in 1939 the Bedford Company had introduced the O Series with a specific model that was factory built to accept the Scammell coupling. This was the **OSS** model (**O** Series, **S** short wheelbase, **S** Scammell coupling). Although few were built before the Second World War, numerous square-bonneted OXC/Scammell units served the armed forces during the war. It must be noted though that the most well known wartime articulated combination, the Queen Mary trailers for the movement of aircraft fuselage and wings, were built by Taskers and fitted with Taskers own style of semi-permanent coupling. When Bedford were able to commence sales to civilian operators after the war, the OSS model entered serious production and the 'O' Series range of vehicles rapidly became the market leader in rigid and articulated form.

Of course, the Bedford name remained at the forefront offering, after 1950, the renowned S Series truck, colloquially known as the 'Big Bedford'. One particular version was used as the basis for an articulated tractor, known as the **SA** model. This brand new model, like its brother the A or TJ bonneted model, brought a brand new style of cab, being loosely based on American General Motors truck design. The Bedford-Scammell connection carried on into the TK range from 1960 onwards, with factory-modified KGA or KHA chassis that were sent to Watford to have the coupling gear fitted. As well as being the first mass producer to fit Scammell couplings to its chassis, the Bedford Company was also to offer the final mass-produced lorry chassis to be fitted with the Scammell coupling, the TK and its successor the TL. The TL tractor model was engineered to receive a Scammell coupling and if the customer required a fifth wheel coupling, then the chassis had to receive a substantial subframe to bring the fifth wheel up to a suitable height.

The Bedford S Series of lorries was introduced to replace the well known O Series. The S featured the first forward control cab built by the company in the United Kingdom for normal road use. With the close ties between Bedford and Scammell a short-wheelbase tractor was available, known as the SA version. The chassis frame was substantially modified to fit the Scammell coupling as can be seen from the downward curve of the chassis members behind the cab. *(Courtesy Colin Green)*

British Insulated Callendar's Cables in Leigh, Lancashire were enthusiastic users of Scammell automatic couplings. Seen here is a 1953 Leyland Comet coupled to a standard straight-framed Scammell dropside trailer with two very carefully positioned cable drums showing the manufacturers name in the correct position. *(Courtesy BICC Ltd)*

This photographs depict two brand new tractor units, Bedford A4 and Scarab 6-ton, complete with a JEKTA ejector trailer. These sectional trailer bodies were built by Walkers of Wigan and used a hydraulic ram to push the load out of the trailer, telescoping the sections as the ram extended. This principle overcame the problem of trailers tipping over sideways if the load stuck whilst the body was raised to discharge the load. This design also allowed the load to be ejected in areas of restricted headroom. Today, exactly the same principle is used by modern dustcarts to discharge their load.

Peacetime Developments

After the war the basic Scammell coupling gear could be supplied direct to truck manufacturers for them to fit in their own production lines, rather than require the tractor to travel to Watford to have the equipment fitted. From photographic evidence, Thornycroft at Basingstoke and Guy in Wolverhampton certainly made use of this facility.

Many Mechanical Horses were bought for use in industrial premises where their ultimate manoeuvrability and ease of exchanging loaded and empty trailers was essential in the days before the wholesale introduction of fork lift trucks and the associated palletisation of goods.

The Scammell and Karrier marketing policies of the mid-thirties to the high quality, well established own account operators, plus the ever increasing fleet of vehicles operated by the railway companies, gave a very high profile to the Scammell product and meant that the benefits of the automatic coupling principle were seen by many haulage operators as an ideal tool to increase flexibility within their operations whilst also offering reduced costs. Possibly the use of the Scammell coupling system by the armed forces during the war, and later, introduced many drivers and managers to the potential of the system in haulage work.

As the obvious advantages of the automatic coupling came to the notice of the road transport industry after the war a number of truck manufacturers came to offer a chassis that was suitable for conversion to an articulated tractor with a Scammell coupling. The manufacturer most closely associated with Scammell remained Bedford, whose motto 'you see them everywhere' was very appropriate for the foremost manufacturer of medium size trucks in the United Kingdom.

Vauxhall Motors had built almost half a million Bedford trucks by 1947, admittedly around half of that total had been built in wartime, but large numbers of Bedford trucks from the 1932-34 period were still in use. Only Ford could even consider themselves as competitors to Bedford as far as mass production was concerned, though by the late forties the V8 petrol engined 7V model was somewhat long in the tooth and few, if any, received Scammell couplings.

Mass produced trucks from Austin, Commer and Dodge had a loyal customer base and numbers of their trucks journeyed to Watford to receive automatic couplings. Additionally, the 'hand-built' trucks offered by the small independent manufacturers like Dennis, Seddon and Thornycroft, though relatively expensive, sold well to a variety of operators looking for unusual specifications and longevity and many received Scammell couplings. Of the heavy duty premium truck manufacturers, at the end of the 1940s, only the Albion marque was able or willing to supply suitable chassis for automatic coupling fitting.

Strangely enough, Ford was very slow in offering chassis suitable for use as tractor units. The Fordson 7V was occasionally modified to pull trailers and the later Thames 500E models could be seen with Brockhouse, Carrimore or BTC trailers using various forms of fifth wheel couplings. It was not until Ford introduced their ground-breaking Trader in 1959 that the short wheelbase tractor unit became a regular production option, although the chassis still required substantial modification at the Scammell works to suit the automatic coupling equipment.

Those companies that came to make up BMC, notably Austin and Morris, oddly enough did not offer a factory built chassis suitable for conversion until the normal-control Loadstar model was in production. The later forward-control BMC Austin/Morris Series III 7-ton models, however, became a very popular base for conversion to a tractor unit with the chassis being specifically built to accept the automatic coupling gear, this model becoming very popular. Most of the tractor units at the time had a wheelbase between 7ft 6in and 8ft 0in and the short wheelbase combined with stiff springing guaranteed a lively ride for the driver when the unit was solo or coupled with an unladen trailer.

The automatic coupling gear soon came to be fitted to virtually all manufacturers' trucks offering up to 12-tons payload, the middleweight Albion, BMC, Bedford, Commer and Ford ranges were the main users. The most common load capacity was 8-10 tons and only latterly did the 12-ton payload become the norm, all on single axle trailers. Automatic coupled Dennis, Guy, Seddon and Thornycroft tractors were seen in small numbers. With the take-over of Scammell by Leyland in 1955, ever-increasing numbers of their Comet range received Watford-built coupling gear with

The establishment of British Road Services in 1948 brought a large number of Scammell-fitted tractor units into the fleet. By the mid-fifties many of the older tractor units needed replacing and Dodge Motors supplied a number of their normal control 124A/P6 models to BRS including this one destined for the North Norfolk Group of BRS. The photograph was taken outside University Coachworks in Cambridge where the trailer body may have been built and the whole unit painted.

An amusing tale surrounds this photograph. When originally published for advertising purposes the background was not totally clear, but the inference from the Scammell advertising caption was that the Scarab 6 export model with twin headlights was photographed in Copenhagen. This copy goes to show that photographs can lie. The photo was taken outside the Artichoke Public House on Croxley Green near Watford and the real giveaway is the London Transport (green country bus) set of timetables on the pub wall!!

The town of Grimsby has long been associated with the manufacture of frozen foods, stemming from the need to process fish caught by trawlers based in Grimsby. Amongst many manufacturers was Eskimo Frozen Foods who made use of this 6-ton Scarab, built in 1959, to transfer products between factories.

This nicely signwritten mobile shop belonged to the Musselburgh Co-operative Society in Midlothian. Based on a 6/8-ton drop-frame trailer the body was almost certainly built by the Scottish Co-operative Wholesale Society works at nearby Leith. It was generally hauled by a Bedford OSS tractor unit, which no doubt left the trailer on site whilst it carried out other important work.

The South Western Gas Board placed this 6-ton Scarab registered PYA 10 on duty at Taunton Gas Works in 1953. Its main responsibilities would have been the transport of bulk coal and coke supplies to and from the gas works. The coal would have been brought from the local rail sidings for the production of gas. The coke was a by-product from the manufacture of town gas and was sold locally to domestic and industrial users for heating and steam generating purposes. Note the scorch marks on the side of the coke hopper where red hot coke discharged directly from the retorts had caught fire, a fairly regular occurrence within gas works at that time.

From the mid-thirties Karrier Motors were able to fit their own version of the Scammell automatic coupling to both their Cob three-wheel and Bantam four-wheel tractor units. The Bantam was originally built with a wooden-framed cab, but from the very early 50s was available with a version of the steel cab fitted to the Commer forward control models. The Bantam was able to offer a little more stability than the three-wheel Scammell units and one is seen here coupled to a mobile gas showroom, built by S H Bond of Wythenshawe near Manchester and operated by the North West Gas Board. This showroom exhibited the latest models of gas cookers, heaters and fires and could also accept payment for gas bills. It was later converted into a mobile office.

many supplied to the nationalised concerns like British Road Services, BRS Parcels and British Railways. Of the Albion range, the Chieftain and Clydesdale chassis were regularly being sent to Watford to receive Scammell couplings. At this time companies like AEC, Atkinson, ERF, Foden and Leyland tended to promote long life, heavy-duty 8-wheel trucks rather than articulated models at 10-15-tons gross weight and only very few of these manufacturers fitted Scammell automatic couplings. Small numbers of AEC Mercury tractor models with a special short wheelbase were built for BRS with Scammell couplings, whilst even fewer lighter weight Atkinson and the odd Foden tractors had the benefit of automatic coupling.

Certainly by the 1950s it seemed that almost every self respecting transport company owned at least one Scammell articulated combination. The benefits of automatic coupling were already accepted as a major advantage by many thousands of C licence operators. These companies, who could only carry their own goods, made use of the previously-stated fact that whilst one trailer was being loaded a second trailer could be unloading and a third in transit, all served by one tractor unit.

The automatic coupling soon became equally popular within the 'for hire and reward' haulage sector where vehicles operated under A or B licences. In simple terms, the A licence enabled a haulier to carry goods anywhere, but the licences were difficult to obtain with the haulier having to prove a specific need for a licence. Interestingly, the railway companies and British Railways were bitterly opposed to the granting of any additional road vehicle licences since they could take potential traffic away from the railway freight operation. The B licence was far more restrictive in that it generally specified the type of goods to be carried and very often the small area in which the vehicle could work.

Many hauliers realised, just like the own account (C licenced) operators before the war, that driver productivity could be greatly increased by exchanging trailers. The simplest format could involve separate three-wheel tractor units collecting and delivering goods in crowded towns and passing the loaded trailer to a four-wheel tractor for the trunk journey. Other operators used the articulation system to exchange trunking trailers at pre-arranged central locations between home-based tractor units. Many more relied on

the use of three or more trailers per unit to ensure that the tractor unit was fully occupied. This system was certainly employed at many docks and warehouses where trailers could be left for loading at the convenience of the dock labour force. Back to Scammell for another comment . . .

It is an oft-quoted fact that for every tractor unit fitted with a Scammell automatic coupling at least two trailers would also be supplied.

This was the period before the advent of palletisation, unit loads and fork lift trucks. Only the humble sack barrow and human muscle was available to load vehicles, hence loading took a long time. This was fertile territory for trailer manufacturers since the less costly trailers could be left on site to be loaded or unloaded whilst the expensive tractor unit was out on delivery with another.

Right through the 1950s and into the mid-1960s the automatic coupling remained in great favour. The British Trailer Company (BTC), Brockhouse (Marks I-III) Hands G-types and Taskers – amongst others – brought out alternative versions of the coupling and most were more or less compatible and interchangeable. Rather like the Karrier coupling design of the 1930s the couplings used by Hands and Taskers both utilised C shaped clamps to hold the flanged wheels in place.

All of the coupling gear would look similar, but had a number of differences, mainly involved with the design and look of the coupling ramps themselves. For instance, Taskers used a fabricated beam under the trailer turntable compared with a cast beam on the Scammell models. The overall payload of the trailers was gradually increased by all the makers to 12-tons and undercarriages were modified so as not to collapse or retract on uncoupling. This had always been a potential problem with Scammell couplings that were not regularly serviced and greased. Taskers were the first to promote their 'Fail Safe' design, using a rigid undercarriage and smaller landing wheels on the coupling.

There was a further version of the Scammell coupling built by Brockhouse, which looked similar, but was totally incompatible and will be referred to later. The old established Carrimore Company had brought out their own version of an easily coupled tractor/trailer unit called the 'Retractor'. This design had flat lead-on ramps and a version of the fifth wheel turntable, the

Seddon vehicles were a comparative rarity amongst brewery vehicles, but this 1956 model with a frameless semi-trailer tank and Scammell coupling shows that Whitbread were not afraid to try the unknown!.

This A Series Bedford was fitted with Bedford's own diesel engine in place of the standard petrol engine. The Bedford A Series were introduced in 1953, but used a style of cab dating back to an American design of 1947. In this case the complete unit was used for the delivery of bagged coke from Ipswich Gas Works. *(Courtesy National Grid)*

Inter-works transport was a speciality of the early Mechanical Horses and Scarabs followed in the same vein. Where factories and suppliers had widely spaced production units the tractor units could work with three or more trailers, with one being loaded, one in transit and one being unloaded. Part of this operation can be seen here in Slough where an Ivers-Lee-owned 6-ton Scarab is involved in delivering packaging products to the nearby Aspro factory.

Although the Co-operative Societies were renowned for the number of mobile shops they operated on new housing estates, there were always some local companies who offered the same service. Bolton-based Hanburys used this 3-ton Scarab and it is recorded as being the first mobile shop to have operated in Bolton. Hanbury's themselves operated a number of retail outlets across the whole of Manchester and surrounding district and lasted into the 1990s when they closed in the face of unremitting competition from larger retailers.

trailer landing gear was fitted one third of the way down the chassis and looked like a pair of modern landing legs that folded backwards as the trailer coupled to the tractor. In theory this design was only sold to companies who were entering the articulated market for the first time and the fact that this system was incompatible with others designs did not matter.

Hundreds of haulage companies, manufacturing and even Government operations like the General Post Office and the Army came to rely on automatic coupling trailers. The motor manufacturing companies in the Midlands were enthusiastic users of the system with their numerous separate manufacturing units supplying a centralised production line. The ability to have spare trailers acting as mobile store rooms certainly helped smooth out supply and production problems.

To gain some idea of the popularity of the Scammell system one only has to look at road traffic photographs or films of this period to see that invariably a Scammell combination will appear somewhere in the background. The one simple clue to look for on these auto-coupling trailers is the complete absence of landing legs on the trailer, because, of course, the auto coupling landing legs were nicely tucked up out of harms way above the tractor unit' rear axle.

Primarily designed for short haul work the Scammell units came to be used as trunk vehicles in their own right giving a very cost effective 8-ton unit for not much more than the cost of a 4-tonner. Despite the trailers` basic simplicity there were certainly problems that only manifested themselves after considerable use. The brass to brass electrical contacts between tractor and trailer would tend to wear and if an unladen trailer was driven along a bumpy road then the rear lights would tend to go on and off as the contacts moved relative to each other. The complicated trailer undercarriage with numerous joints and links would become very loose, the jaws and brake connections on both tractor and trailer were also subject to wear, especially when the trailers were frequently coupled and uncoupled. Another interesting fault came about if the tractor and trailer were only infrequently disconnected and the trailer undercarriage had not been regularly lubricated. As the tractor unit drove away from the trailer, the undercarriage would fail to 'unlock' and the trailer would fall on its knees!

From the earliest versions of the Scammell coupling there had always been a separate handbrake in the tractor cab for the trailer brakes, enabling a driver to slow down just using the trailer brakes; this type of braking kept the trailer in line behind the unit and reduced the risk of jack-knifing. The numerous brake linkages (cables, levers and rods) between the driver's brake pedal and the brake actuation on the trailer meant that as the units aged there was a definite time lag in trailer brake application and this could bring about instability on braking. There was little possibility of closely matching the braking capabilities of tractor and trailer, especially in a fleet with different weights and sizes of semi-trailer so a separate independent trailer brake was a vital item for the driver.

In 1958 the Brockhouse Company brought out their Mark IV version of the coupling gear which remained compatible with existing automatic couplings, but had an interesting braking concept. This featured a Clayton Dewandre Hydrovac suspended vacuum servo to eliminate the delay in actuation of the trailer brakes previously referred to. If the trailer brakes are applied fractionally before the tractor unit's brakes it helps keep the complete combination in a straight line and reduces the chance of a jack-knife incident. In theory this removed the need for the driver to operate the trailer handbrake whilst braking under normal road conditions.

Often other trailer manufacturers would buy the Scammell coupling gear and trailer axles to put under their own chassis. This process seemed mainly to be used by British Railways in the fifties when they no doubt sent out tenders for the supply of perhaps 200 complete van trailers fitted with Scammell coupling and Scammell had declined to tender due to production problems thereby allowing others to build the trailers.

The range of trailers and bodies in use was absolutely remarkable: from box vans to flats, from furniture vans to step frames and from fridge vans to pole carriers. In fact, if it was not in the catalogue then Scammell would simply design one for you; it is generally accepted that the 'standard' range of Scammell trailers comprised about 600 different types! Not forgetting of course that the originators of the principle, the railways, were buying these trailers by the thousand. Within the

A North West Gas Board Morris Commercial FV Series II tractor unit fitted with a Scammell coupling is shown being loaded with coke bags for domestic delivery in Manchester. *(Courtesy Transco National Gas Archive)*

One of the many BMC tractor units fitted with Scammell coupling gear, was this 1954 Morris Seies 3 articulated tractor, operated from the Morris factory in Oxford.

A busy scene at Kings Cross (London) British Railway goods yard showing an almost new 3-ton Scarab about to leave on a delivery journey with a very mixed load of packages. In those days, not only did the goods have to withstand being handled many times, they also had to be waterproof as the trailers had little weatherproofing. However, the advantage of open trailers was that access to all parts of the load was easy and the drivers were supplied with tarpaulins to cover the load in inclement weather.

The industrial uses that Scammell Scarabs were put to is verified by this photo of a 6-ton model with tipping trailer at the works of Monsanto Chemicals near Wrexham.

Heavy cable drums were amongst the more difficult loads to handle. Here a drum is being hand winched onto a drop frame Scammell trailer. The rear wheels of the trailer have been removed as was normal with this type of operation and the trailer bed lowered to ground level, using mechanical jacks. *(Courtesy BICC Ltd)*

Here a 3-ton British Railways Scarab based at Berkhampstead in Hertfordshire is about to undertake a delivery run to the Kings Arms public house with a load of Bass beer from Burton on Trent. At that time in the mid-fifties British Railways were a major carrier of beer across the country.

railway fleet alone one could find the following trailer types:

Flat platforms,

Dropsides,

Tippers,

Extendable platforms,

Pole trailers,

Half tilt vans,

Full tilt vans,

Vanesta bodies

(these were wire mesh sided bodies),

Glass carriers,

Drop frame and step frame trailers of various types,

Cable drum carriers

Plus a huge variety of vans of differing sizes and door positions.

Amongst the most interesting regular production offerings came the frameless tankers.

Built exactly as the name suggests the tank itself acted as the chassis frame and the coupling gear and axles were mounted directly on the tank shell. This gave quite a weight saving over a conventional articulated tanker and became very popular with the petrol companies. The tank shells generally would have been supplied to Scammell's by outside contractors like Butterfields of Shipley and Thompson Brothers (Bilston) Ltd.

It would take a further volume of this book to describe the variety of operators, vehicle and trailer combinations involved, but the reader can be assured that the companies making use of the automatic coupling designed by OD North had penetrated virtually every spectrum of British industry from international road haulage to internal works transport.

Looking slightly the worse for wear is this mid-fifties Dennis Horla tractor unit owned by the Manchester operation of the Co-operative Wholesale Society. A full load of empty cases and pallets is carried on the 20ft long flat trailer. *(A Ingram)*

GSU Information

GSU were closely connected with Grahams in Manchester and established as a separate company, GSU standing for either Graham Scammell Units or Grahams Service Units and trading as a Scammell Trailers main dealer, handling the sales of new and used Scammell Mechanical Horses and later Scarabs and Townsman. In addition, they sold new and second-hand four-wheel tractor units that had been fitted with Scammell automatic coupling conversions.

In 1946 Graham Brothers decided to establish an 'articulated vehicle sales operation' and Mr Saxon Hill was sent to their Chester Road, Manchester depot to establish the operation. As part of the training process in selling Scammell trailers, Mr Hill was sent to Scammell's Watford factory to learn all about the vehicles. The training course involved learning how to drive and couple/uncouple trailers fitted with automatic couplings. The trainees were given an old three-wheel Mechanical Horse and a trailer carrying a full load of concrete blocks. When the time came for the trainees to uncouple the trailer the instructor said

"well I'll just stand outside and observe", leaving the trainee to pull the uncoupling lever in the cab and to drive slowly away. What the instructor had not told the trainees was that as the loaded trailer was released from its coupling, it would literally shoot the tractor forward from under the trailer, to the great surprise of the trainee, who of course hit his head on the cab roof, much to the amusement of the instructor!

Incidentally, in the 1930s, railway drivers of previously horse drawn drays would come to the Watford factory of Scammell Lorries on conversion courses to learn to drive motor vehicles. These drivers could quite frequently be heard to shout "whoa!" as they headed straight for the wall at the controls of an unfamiliar three-wheeled petrol-powered MH tractor unit.

GSU sold large numbers of Scammell trailers in the North West along with hundreds of Scammell three-wheelers and Scammell-converted four-wheel tractors. There was also a thriving business in supplying reconditioned trailer coupling gear. Despite the apparent simplicity of the Scammell automatic coupling, the actual engineering was quite complex with a lot of moving, and therefore,

No doubt originally based in Nottingham, this Bedford A Series tractor unit owned by British Waterways and fitted with a Scammell coupling is seen being loaded with grain at a waterside warehouse. This view shows how easy it is to distinguish automatic coupling trailers from fifth wheel coupling versions, by the complete absence of trailer landing legs.

During the early 1960s British Railways established a number of Freight Concentration Depots across the country. One was built at Walsall to handle specific types of steel destined for the Midlands, the depot was served by direct train loads from steel producing centres. For steel deliveries a railway-owned, Scammell-coupling-fitted, Dennis Horla tractor was among the fleet used.

The Austin/BMC WE and WF Series normal control tractor units remained popular with British Railways through the 1950s and 60s. One is depicted here being loaded with a road/rail BD container by a Pagefield crane, built by the Walker Company of Wigan, at Marylebone goods yard in London.

Taken at Spekelands British Railways goods depot in Liverpool, this animated scene shows incoming goods being placed directly into rail vans for forwarding on to other depots. The variety of goods being handled will be noted, along with their shapes and sizes, and the quality of their packaging.

Just to give an idea of the scope of the British Railways 'sundries' or small goods operation, this photograph was taken at Stoke on Trent and is remarkable for the number of Watford-built Scarabs and trailers plus one Karrier Bantam interloper! The carefully packaged goods are, of course, pottery items manufactured locally.

A somewhat run down Thornycroft Nippy tractor unit complete with Swindon-designed wooden framed Safety Cab' at work in Cardiff in the mid fifties. *(S Vickery)*

A pair of Shelvoke and Drewry Freightlifter fork lift trucks are loading overhead crane rails onto a Scammell fitted BMC 501 tractor unit and 10 ton trailer. The load is destined for Aberthaw Power Station and was photographed at Llantwit Major in 1965. *(S Vickery)*

The Penman Ramp system was originally designed for farmers who needed a simple system to remove demountable livestock transporter bodies from flat platform lorries. The system was demonstrated to British Railways as an alternative means of removing containers from railway wagons and onto flat road trailers. Though simple and cheap to install, to use it in a busy goods yard would entail much shunting of railway wagons.

Despite the introduction of quite modern dustcarts in the late 1950s, the Borough of Wandsworth in London invested in a small fleet of articulated waste collectors based on 6-ton Scammell Scarab tractor units with step-frame trailers complete with power-operated moving floor taking the form of a large rubber belt. Dustbins were emptied into the rear of the vehicle and the rubber belt or conveyor was gradually wound forward as the vehicle continued on its round. When full the conveyor was simply wound backwards to discharge the load.

wearing parts. As a result a complete department of GSU was established to refurbish the couplings for local users and other Scammell dealers across the country.

In later years there was a good deal of uprating the brakes on the trailers from simple mechanical to vacuum or air braking as the Plating and Testing rules for commercial vehicles came into operation in 1968. The new Regulations insisted that all articulated vehicles had to be fitted with primary, secondary and emergency brakes. This entailed the fitting of dual-brake chambers to the trailer axles to operate the foundation drum brakes, leaving the original rod operated brake as the emergency brake. Alterations to the tractor unit involved the installation of additional brake valves and their associated controls.

In the latter years of the 1960s GSU built up a large fleet of trailers for hire; some trailers had been owned by GSU, and a large fleet was taken over from Central Trailers (who were owned by Pitt Trailers). Later the very considerable GSU hire fleet was taken over by Tiphook trading as TIP. It would appear that most of these trailers were fitted with contemporary fifth wheel couplings rather than the automatic coupling designed by Scammell. This business continues today, though the company name has changed, indeed trailer hire or contract hire is a huge business throughout the United Kingdom.

The main benefits of automatic coupling remained with the ease and speed of changing over trailers and the wide variety of trailers available. The overall design of the coupling gear hardly changed over a fifty-year period. Obviously materials improved, and better manufacturing methods were found, but even today a 1933 trailer will couple to a 1970s tractor. The trailer layout hardly changed either, most trailers remained fitted with just a single axle, the Scammell version of which was slightly cambered and was designed to ensure that the wheels remained parallel to the road when the trailer was fully laden.

Brakes on the trailer remained cable and rod operated from the turntable to the axle until the advent of the plating regulations which required additional secondary braking facilities, with air or vacuum operating cylinders being mounted on the trailer axle in addition to those on the tractor unit. This, of course, meant that the driver had to leave his cab to couple up the air or vacuum lines, but the actual coupling operation still remained quick and simple. During the late 'sixties Scammell introduced the Mark 3 coupling gear that featured a retractable, but non-collapsible undercarriage and was fitted with much smaller landing wheels, this undercarriage was very similar to those built by Hands and Taskers which had been introduced a little earlier.

Back in the 1930s, a number of Mechanical Horses had been exported to Australia in CKD (completely-knocked-down) format which would be assembled by the local Scammell distributors. Sales of these vehicles continued after the war and the Scarab model was sold complete with trailers. The Australian market soon demanded a different type of trailer that was more torsionally rigid than the British models, and these were manufactured locally. The heavy duty Mark 3 Scammell coupling introduced in the 1970s did not suit the locally built trailers and the Australian distributors made their own version to suit the local market. This revised coupling was fitted to Isuzu medium weight tractor units up till the mid 1980s, but by then heavier payload requirements were making the automatic coupling far less competitive and the Australian distributor closed down in 1988.

Even though Scammell had built a number of 24-ton automatic coupling gears on Highwayman tractors from 1950 onwards they had never been the expected commercial success. The initial heavy-duty couplings were loosely based on the original design of automatic coupling, with the king pin mounted on the tractor chassis turntable base rather than more common SAE system used by other manufacturers. A little later a modified version was made available with just the top half of the trailer coupling running up the tractor ramps.

The impressive feature of these larger couplings was that they utilised air brakes that coupled automatically and that air pressure was also used to raise and lower the landing legs that were separate from the coupling gear. These large automatic couplings were seen by Scammell as an alternative to their existing heavy-duty fifth wheel coupling which was not compatible with the fifth wheel couplings coming into in general use. However, by the early sixties Scammell could see that they required a standard fifth wheel coupling design of their own and set about manufacturing one that could be fitted to heavier articulated vehicles that operated at 24-tons gross and these were fitted to Leyland Group vehicles as well as articulated tractors manufactured by outside companies.

At this point we must briefly look at one effect that the earlier Leyland take-over had on the small tractor units built at Watford. The Karrier Bantam tractor had one advantage over the existing Scarab three-wheeled tractor unit in that it was deemed a little more stable. Leyland Motors then decided to bring out a competitor to Karrier in the form of the Scarab Four.

In 1961 Leyland had taken over the Standard Company and this enabled the Scammell engineers to develop a small tractor unit to compete with the Bantam by joining the front end of the existing Standard Atlas van to the rear end of the Scammell Scarab 3-ton chassis, theoretically providing a four-wheel tractor unit with a roomy cab and the engine placed behind the cab, hopefully providing a quiet working place for the driver. This new model was announced at the 1962 Earls Court Commercial Show, but production did not commence until 1964. A road test of a complete Scarab Four and trailer was undertaken when the tester was impressed by the general performance, manoeuvrability and stability, but it was 'less than happy when being pushed hard and when cruising at 35/40mph it was noisy'. The single reduction rear axle enabled a maximum speed of 44mph to be attained, but it was then described as 'unbearably noisy with everything vibrating fit to burst'. Added to these comments were the problems of enormous cab doors making access and egress from the cab difficult in restricted areas. Other complaints included the facts that the driver's eyeline was above the windows, the cab was not as roomy as promised. Ventilation was poor and the view rearwards when reversing was inadequate, as the cab door window did not open enough for the driver to lean out.

Unfortunately, the Scarab Four was one of the very few Scammell products to be deemed a complete failure. The only large order was for about 100 examples to be delivered to the South African Railway operation and only a further handful were sold in the United Kingdom. It was soon dropped from production.

The automatic coupling with all its inherent advantages of ease of use, simplicity and speed remained popular for some 40 years. However,

with the introduction of heavier gross vehicle weights in the 1960s and a realisation within the nationalised British Railways that their road operations were not profitable, an irreversible change in the use of automatic couplings took place. The first alteration was the demise of the Scarab and the Karrier Bantam and other small articulated units which started in the early to middle-sixties. This happened when British Railways set about modernising their sundries collection and delivery services to cope with a continuing disastrous loss of traffic and minimal profitability. Many outlying depots were closed and delivery routes lengthened from the remaining depots and these required larger rigid vehicles with a greater load capacity and higher speeds, with vehicles completing just one journey per day. There was no need for the exchange of trailers during a day's work and thus less need for new small articulated tractors.

Under the 1968 Transport Act, the British Railways Sundries Division was passed to the nationalised National Freight Corporation, which was essentially a road-based freight handling operation, with British Road Services as another constituent of the NFC. The Sundries Division was re-branded as 'National Carriers', still working out of railway associated sites, but gradually the rail links between depots were replaced by road trunking operations. The parcels operation of British Road Services was re-named 'Roadline'.

Another blow was that the new Plating and Testing Regulations appeared to threaten the very existence of three-wheel tractor units with unbraked front wheels. Trials had been carried out in Scammell's Experimental Department as to the possibility of building a three-wheeler tractor unit with front brakes. Various assessments were carried out using brake equipment from Rootes Group cars, and overall the trials had a successful outcome, giving a higher quality of braking, although it remained vital that the braking effort was proportioned correctly to prevent the whole unit and trailer becoming unstable. These were the days before load sensing valves were available to reduce braking effort on lightly laden axles.

It was decided not to go ahead with the plan to either build new three-wheelers with front brakes or even to retrofit any existing vehicles. The logic behind the decision was almost certainly that both Scammell and British Railways realised that the heyday of the three-wheeler was almost over. The

Many trailers looking outwardly like the products of the Watford factory of Scammell Lorries were in fact built by other manufacturers, but used a Scammell undercarriage to ensure compatibility with existing tractor units. This 8-10 ton dropside trailer was in fact built by Taskers in Andover for the British Aluminium Company in Bootle. *(Courtesy Taskers Trailers)*

Amongst the amazing range of standard trailers built by Scammell Lorries were the extending pole carriers for long lengths of steel or timber. Because they only had a central spine chassis they were liable to twist when uncoupled from the tractor unit, hence the fitting of additional landing wheels just behind the undercarriage.

Newcastle on Tyne haulier J W Capstaff operated this Guy Warrior fitted with automatic coupling. The cab made use of a standard Motor Panels design with the Guy Company supplying the cab base. *(RN Hannay)*

A 1958 photograph showing a nicely lined up fleet of Ulster Ferry Transport Guy Warrior tractor units fitted with Meadows 4DC330 diesel engines and Brockhouse couplings suitable for use with Scammell automatic coupling trailers. The gross train weight of the vehicles was 15½ tons. These tractor units were later replaced by Leyland Comet tractor units. Ulster Ferry Transport were responsible for the delivery of a full range of goods to Ulster for industrial, retail and domestic customers. *(RN Hannay)*

Just in case we were not sure of the make of this vehicle, the manufacturer, Guy Motors, stencilled the model name on the cab rear panel, prior to this Scammell-fitted tractor unit being delivered to a main dealer for painting in an operators livery. This overhead view clearly shows the Scammell coupling with the twin hooks and spring-loaded buffers to hold the trailer coupling in position. The steel tongue which made the trailer undercarriage retract is seen behind the differential. The rear light assemblies are slid into position and can easily be moved onto the trailer when required. *(RN Hannay)*

Amongst the many goods vehicles operated by London Transport to keep their buses on the road was this Thames Trader tractor unit with this very tidy looking York single axle trailer used for the distribution of new tyres to bus and coach garages. *(Courtesy M Clark)*

The Hampshire registration on this 3-ton Scammell Scarab gives a clue that it Scammell Scarab was operated from the Courage brewery at Alton. The Scarab was used for local beer deliveries, the low height of the trailer deck easing the job of the drayman when moving barrels. This concept of low loading height articulated units has been followed by the 'urban artics' of the late 20th Century based on small wheeled tractor units mainly from the Leyland/DAF, MAN and Volvo ranges.

Although British Railways were to become major users of the final model of the Karrier Bantam, using a version of the Rootes Group cab fitted to the Commer lorry range, a large number were sold into other industries and delivery work, including this 1960 example working for the Kinloch food distribution operation.

Possibly the best remembered Karrier Bantam tractor units are those operated by British Railways and later National Carriers in yellow livery. Here, a 1964 example is seen in Sussex coupled to a Hands 5-ton box van trailer. *(P Love)*

Photographed at the handing over ceremony of the very first Scammell Townsman to be sold are Bert Thomas of Scammell Motors and Roger Steele on the right. This 3-ton Scammell Townsman coupled to a 15ft box van would be used to deliver groceries around Bolton on behalf of E H Steele who traded as General Provision Merchants. The Scammell Townsman was a direct replacement for the 3-ton Scarab and featured a Leyland OE160 diesel engine and a welded chassis as well as a fibreglass cab. Despite orders of over 1,000 Townsman for British Railways and others for the GPO Mail delivery service it was never the success expected since the whole need for small three-wheel articulated vehicles was disappearing by the time this model was introduced.

Quite an anachronism at the time was this Townsman 3-ton refuse collector delivered to Chesterfield in 1965. The basic design of dustcart would be recognised by dustmen of the mid-1930s. It was fitted with a moving floor, with the dustmen simply tipping the rubbish into the back of the body onto a wide rubber conveyor which was wound forward to give more space for loading further wastes. To unload the dustcart, the conveyor was simply wound backwards at the local tip.

cost of fitting these brakes to the existing fleet was just not economically feasible. Had the brakes been fitted to just part of the fleet the braking characteristics would have been so different between otherwise identical vehicles so as to cause the drivers numerous problems.

In the early sixties Scammell planned to update the smaller 3-ton Scarab to produce a three-wheeled tractor unit that could remain in operation into the seventies on the railways sundries division. The outcome was the three-wheeled, fibreglass-cabbed, Scammell Townsman, fitted with the Standard/Leyland OE160 diesel engine and hydraulic brakes, in 1964. The Townsman was to immediately replace the 3-ton Scarab, though production of 6-ton Scarabs continued until 1967.

According to Paul Cooper, who worked on the production line at Scammell's Watford factory, a difficult problem arose when the Scarab, Scarab 4 and Townsman were being produced at the same time. The original Scarab three-wheelers were built with BSF threaded nuts and bolts, whilst the Scarab 4 and Townsman used the more modern UNF fasteners. It was certain that UNF nuts could, in error, be forced onto BSF bolts and vice versa, especially given the fact that many of the chassis build-ups were completed by the apprentices at that time. Some chassis bolts could be finger tight, whilst others were practically at thread stripping point. Luckily, all quality problems were cured by the Road Test Department.

The Townsman attracted reasonably large orders from British Railways and the General Post Office as well as from a number of smaller users. But in reality the day of the three-wheeled articulated tractor, and indeed its small four-wheeled brother in the form of the Karrier Bantam and also the tiny Ford D Series DA600 Baby Artic, was passing.

The second reason for the eventual demise of the automatic coupling, though, followed the general uprating of vehicle gross weights with the 1964 and 1968 Construction and Use Regulations. Under these new rules there was a massive jump towards 32-ton articulated truck operation making use of fifth wheel couplings mandatory with tandem or tri-axle trailers and giving a payload potential of 21/22-tons. This compared with just 12-tons payload which was the very maximum that the regulations considered safe with the automatic coupling. Thus, at a stroke many of the auto coupling's inbuilt advantages were lost despite the popularity of the system. This had a very serious effect on the lifeblood of the Scammell Company with its 'raison d'etre' of the automatic coupling being rapidly outmoded. Of course, Scammell already supplied a fifth wheel coupling that could be fitted to any suitable tractor unit and fifth wheel compatible trailers had been manufactured at Watford for many years, giving the Scammell Company a secure place in the market for heavier trailers.

Interestingly, there was an up-side to the new regulations, though not immediately obvious. There were many haulage operators who had fleets of relatively new Scammell single axle trailers and equally serviceable four-, six- or eight-wheel rigid trucks. It did not take long before Scammell 'dollies' became common place on the roads of the United Kingdom. These dollies were not the two legged variety to be found in certain areas, but a single axle unit with an automatic coupling fitted on it. They fitted neatly under a normal Scammell single axle trailer converting it immediately to a drawbar trailer with a potential payload of 12-tons, enabling it to be towed by existing rigid load carrying lorries, often giving up to 24 or 32-tons gross train weight with existing equipment, purchasing no more than the dolly and a drawbar hook and braking equipment on the drawing unit.

There was an interesting sideline on these conversions when the Police (possibly in London) attempted to prove that a lorry plus dolly plus trailer meant that the lorry was towing two trailers, which was illegal. After going to court the haulier was found not guilty, with the police case sensibly being thrown out.

With the new Vehicle Plating regulations, all articulated combinations had to be fitted with both primary and secondary braking systems. The original Scammell coupling had just a single brake system consisting of a pair of rod operated brakes on the trailer axle, connection from the tractor unit was through the centre of the coupling with a further mechanical linkage to the rear axle. To continue to operate after 1968 all trailers had to be fitted with an additional braking system. Unfortunately, the introduction of vacuum or air braking systems to the automatic coupling immediately removed one of the major selling points of the coupling, ie no need for any action

For many years the GPO (General Post Office) had been users of products from the Watford factory of Scammell Lorries. Both the postal and telephone services used automatic coupling vehicles. This Morris FFK is shown with a specialised cable drum carrying trailer, built by Taskers which has a suspension system based on that developed for the 'Queen Mary' wartime aircraft trailer fuselage carriers. *(Courtesy Taskers Trailers)*

This short wheelbase Dennis Pax was converted into a battery-powered tractor unit and coupled to a rear loading refuse trailer for use with the City of Westminster for rubbish collection.

Photographed at the Lincoln premises of Ruston Gas Turbines in 1981 this Scammell Townsman dates from 1966. As can be ascertained by the large number of trailers in the background, this Townsman, along with 3-ton Scarabs, had seen busy times moving material between machine shops and the assembly areas.

Photographs of Scammell Townsman tractors at work with National Carriers are fairly rare. The author took this photo in Wembley in 1970 of a Townsman complete with two small wheeled 1-ton SW containers which could easily be transferred from road to rail wagon in the days before palletisation was fully accepted by all customers.

A 1966 Scammell Townsman is photographed leaving a London Midland Region goods depot with a nicely tarpaulined load. At this time all goods drivers were paid a bonus on the weight of goods delivered, hence the regular call to the weighbridge office.

A 1967 Bedford TK 8-10 ton tractor unit showing how little the basic concept of the Scammell coupling had changed in the previous 34 years. The only noticeable alteration is the addition of an electrical cable to operate the trailer lights instead of the earlier brass contacts and the fact that the rear lights of the tractor unit are now permanently attached rather than having to be transferred to the trailer. The cab of the Bedford TK range of vehicles was not designed to tilt for maintenance, instead hinged flaps behind both cab doors allowed mechanics access to the engine compartment.

Built in 1947, Bedford OSS EED 510 was a second-hand tractor sold by GSU in Manchester to LORCO, the London Oil Refining Company. It was originally registered in Warrington, but unfortunately the original owner is unknown. The location of the photograph is Ancoats in Manchester and a Manchester Corporation Crossley style bodied bus can be seen in the background. The granite setts and gas lamps make this a real period picture. The transport manager of Lorco had served in the Army with Mr Saxon Hill from GSU.

Demonstrating the remarkable lock available from the front wheel is a 6-ton Scammell Mechanical Horse, ready for delivery from GSU to Anderton & Sons of Ardwick, Manchester. Although the vehicle was built post war, the 2 litre petrol engine still needed to be started by hand. Andertons were paper merchants in Manchester and the MD was a personal friend of the local Scammell salesman Bert Thomas. It was very difficult to drive a Mechanical Horse away with the front wheel at that angle, even in the low first gear, it was necessary to straighten the steering first.

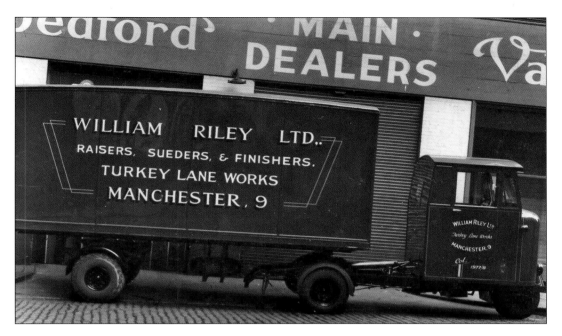

Looking like a normal 3-ton Mechanical Horse, this specimen, about to be delivered to William Riley Ltd from GSU, was in fact a 3/6-ton model with twin rear wheels and capable of pulling a six ton load, even though the coupling was only the 3-ton version. Depending on the customers specific requirements Scammell would do their best to supply the most appropriate vehicle for the job. Customers could buy 3-ton models with 6-ton engines or vice versa and could fit either size of coupling gear. Note that the two sizes of coupling gear were not compatible. The curved roof line of the trailer is worth noting, it was a pleasing example of the coachbuilders art. Unfortunately, the expense of building similar bodies today is generally prohibitive.

Maddock and Tunnaley were Manchester-based timber importers who used this 1947 Bedford OSS/Scammell combination to collect timber from the Manchester docks. The mobile crane loading the sawn timber is a Jones Super 40, capable of lifting 2-tons.

on the part of the driver whilst coupling. Once the driver had to start to connect flexible brake hoses and electrical connections, part of the simplicity of the Scammell system was lost.

In order to face up to the new Plating and Testing Regulations the Watford based company introduced a conversion kit to enable fifth wheel king pin fitted trailers to couple easily to Scammell Auto Coupling tractors. The kit consisted of a standard fifth wheel attached to a cross member, which carried the two flanged wheels that fitted onto a Scammell auto coupling. The fifth wheel could either remain on the tractor unit or on the trailer or be transferred between other tractors and trailers. While this was a satisfactory short term measure many users of auto couplings gradually changed completely to fifth wheel couplings, often converting existing trailers to the new format as the tractor units were renewed. Eventually, the conversions themselves were phased out as the rapid move to tandem and tri-axle trailers took place.

The use of automatic couplings continued with the National Freight Corporation-owned companies. National Carriers and Roadline (originally British Road Services Parcel Division) through to the late 1970s and with British Railways-owned Rail Express Parcels into the early 1980s. Both companies had originated with British Railways. National Carriers were the old Sundries Division of the railways, whilst Rail Express Parcels were the higher quality passenger rated delivery and collection system that originally made use of dedicated parcel trains to transport the parcels between main stations. Much of Rail Express's work was based on the collection and delivery of parcels destined for home delivery. In fact, the very last Scammell three-wheel tractors in the form of Townsman 3-tonners finished work with REP at Oldham depot in the 1980s.

It is strange to relate that the two last major users of automatic couplings, the originally nationalised National Carriers and Roadline, were to merge and reappear as Lynx Express. Many of their erstwhile 28ft long auto-coupling vans had been rebuilt into tandem axle, single tyred 40ft box vans fitted with fifth wheel couplings.

It appeared that by the 1990s the auto coupling had breathed its last; yet as late as 1997 the British Army were still using AWD TL (as successors to the Bedford TL models) tractor units fitted with Taskers or Hands style couplings, albeit mostly for driver training purposes on the roads of East Yorkshire.

Despite all the problems for the three and four wheeled automatic coupling trailers they did continue to operate in many areas as works hacks or in their original role of short distance shunting of trailers. The last regular use of automatic couplings appeared to be undertaken by a furniture company in Newhaven, and unfortunately that operation ceased in 2000. Today, only a few preserved automatic coupling units remain to show the public what a simple system it was and also to prove what a milestone the system was in the movement towards the general acceptance of the articulation concept.

With the closure of the Scammell factory the trailer manufacturing operation passed to Aveling Barford and then to York Trailers, but the trade name Scammell was to disappear completely by 1990. There had been nothing wrong with the basic concept of automatic coupling; it was just that times had changed. Modern mass produced trucks in the 4-10 tonne range could match many of the better points of the three and smaller four wheel tractors. The modern trucks were cheaper to buy and run and economic considerations made the provision of special under-utilised trailers a difficult purchase decision to justify.

Interestingly, though there remained an area of haulage operations that seemed ideal for small articulated units, this area covered the delivery of beers, wines and spirits. Here a fairly Unionised workforce persuaded the brewers and wholesalers that a low loading platform was essential for the heavy work carried out by the draymen in delivering barrels of beer. The lower the height of the lorry platform, the less likely was the possibility of strains and pulled muscles of the draymen. These Union demands heralded the introduction of 'urban artics'; articulated combinations which featured small-wheeled, small-cabbed four-wheel tractor units, often Leyland Freighter or Volvo FL Series coupled to low profile single axle trailers. They were based very closely on the original Karrier/Scammell concept of small tractors with maximum manoeuvrability and although fitted with fifth wheel couplings carrying out exactly the same style of urban delivery work that the railways were involved in some 70 years ago.

The Bedford OSS model was specially built at the factory with the rear chassis shaped to accept the Scammell coupling gear. With very close liaison between Bedford and Scammell, the tractor and trailer were ideally matched and sold as a complete unit, with the guarantee covering both items. This tractor unit was destined to carry crated soft drinks for most of its life.

Seen in an early 1950s typical Mancunian environment is a 6-ton Scarab complete with a trailer load of bottles in wooden crates. Of interest is the noticeable contrast between the glazed bricks of the hostelry and the dull bricks of the surrounding houses. Unfortunately, Chester's Ales are no longer available, the brewer having been taken over by Threlfalls in 1961 and the brewery subsequently demolished in 1966.

Almost the archetypal local distribution vehicle. A Scammell Scarab 3-ton tractor unit with a curtain-sided trailer able to give easy access to all parts of the load without compromising the shelter from the weather. Unlike modern curtain-sided trailers, the curtains on these vehicles were purely for load protection, only with the introduction of the Boalloy curtainsiders did the curtains become load bearing as well.

The Stockport Industrial & Equitable Co-operative Society used this 6-ton Scammell Scarab on coal deliveries around the town. It replaced a 1931 AEC Mercury and no doubt the driver was delighted to be able to step into the cab rather than having to climb up into the small AEC cab through an even smaller door. The Scarab was an ideal local distribution unit, but was expensive when compared to say a Fordson Thames, but the Scarab was more manoeuvrable than a rigid truck and, of course, could pull alternative trailers.

What looks to be a very classy 6-ton Scarab coupled to a step frame dropside trailer. Quite how long the trailer would remain in this pristine condition when working for a scrap metal merchant is open to conjecture. Very prominent in the picture are the twin reflectors on the trailer, a legal requirement on all vehicles from the early 1950s. It is quite likely that this trailer was destined for the carriage of lightweight alloys at the time. Just possibly the unit may have been involved in the collection of redundant aircraft frames. The Scarab was new to a London operator in 1952 and was sold second-hand to Charles Corry in 1956 for £350 0s 0d.

A positively gleaming 6-ton Scarab which cost £885 0s 0d when new in 1954 and was photographed in a somewhat unprepossessing part of Manchester. Unfortunately, neither Scarab nor the brewery were destined to last into the new Millennium. The trailer was possibly built to carry an 8-ton payload when coupled behind a four-wheel tractor unit, hence the twin wheels.

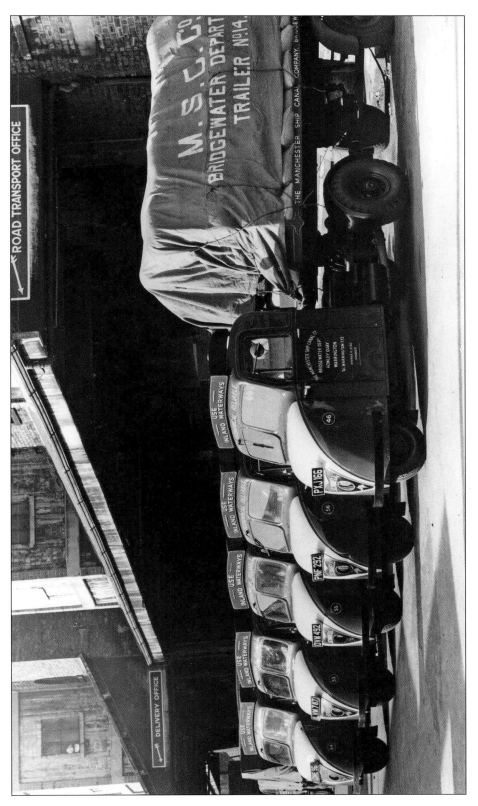

The Manchester Ship Canal Company operated a large number of Scammell coupling tractor units including these 6-ton Scarabs. With a green and cream/white livery they were used to tranship goods from ship to dockside warehouse and occasionally make outside deliveries. In the heyday of Manchester docks much of the merchandise was hand loaded and there was a definite need for 'stand' trailers to wait whilst the goods were loaded. Whilst this was happening the Scarabs would be out working with other trailers. The General Manager of GSU, Mr Saxon Hill, personally sold the large fleets of Scammell automatic coupling trailers to the Ship Canal Company. The second Scarab from the left was a second-hand purchase in 1953 and dated from 1950.

The original design of Bedford SA tractor unit is shown here with a 20 foot long Scammell trailer, fitted with a locally-built dropside body. The Bedford had a wheelbase of 8ft only and a ride in one without a trailer attached was like riding a bucking bronco! Later versions of the SA unit featured a chrome surround to the grille and could be fitted with a diesel engine. The photo was taken in Stockport, possibly in the Reddish area.

New Forge Foods were a division of Lovell & Christmas who were a nationwide grocery wholesaler. This 3-ton Scarab cost £789 10s 0d. when new in 1955 and with its van trailer would have been used for deliveries around the Manchester area to the corner shops and to some of the larger grocery retailers. Many of the corner shops relied on the services of the wholesalers like Lovell & Christmas to deliver goods since the shop owner was unlikely to have owned a car to enable him or her to collect goods. With the general increase in prosperity, car ownership increased, then cash and carry stores opened and this paved the way for the closure of many distribution operations like New Forge Foods.

The Manchester Oil Refinery Company was established in Trafford Park in 1936 for the purpose of manufacturing lubricating and specialised electrical transformer oils. This 6-ton Scammell Scarab would have been used for local deliveries around the Manchester area. The elliptical single compartment trailer tanks were probably discharged by gravity through the bolted flange at the rear of the tank.

Kenkast Ltd were a company based at Lower Green, Astley, Lancashire beside the East Lancashire Road and manufactured concrete-section buildings, especially garages and single storey offices. Part of the delivery fleet is seen here and comprised Bedford T and A Series bonneted articulated tractors along with Bedford SA and an OSS tractor unit. It is likely that the Austin K Series on the far right is fitted with a rigid body. The three Ford 300E vans would have been used by the technical staff for site investigation and possibly promotional purposes. The company commenced operations from a private garage in 1954 and their first delivery vehicle was an old bus (ex-Crosville KA 88, DFM 299, a Leyland TS8 single-decker). The photograph was taken in 1959 when the total fleet of 10 commercials were covering some 10,000 miles weekly. Given the lack of motorways in that period, driving 1,000 miles a week plus site delivery time meant the drivers had to work long hours. In those days, of course, there were no electronic tachographs, just a hand written log book to record where the driver had been.

A fairly early TK tractor unit with a less than aerodynamic headboard, coupled to a 24 foot basic frame trailer fitted with five pressurised tanks for the carriage of bulk beer. The box at the front of the trailer carried gas bottles to charge the tanks to propel the beer on its way from the trailer into the pub cellar tanks.

This British Insulated Callendar's Cables (BICC) Leyland Comet with the LAD cab which was used by Leyland, Albion and Dodge gives an excellent indication of how low the rear chassis frame of a Scammell converted tractor needed to be to accommodate the automatic coupling. The tipper trailer may have been used to bring coal for the works boilers from one of the local south Lancashire collieries, but the tractor unit itself was used for trunking journeys, hence the storage box on the cab roof for tarpaulins. BICC cables were supplied to all the electricity generating and distribution companies across the country. *(Courtesy BICC Ltd)*

With GSU being the main Scammell agent for the North West of England they sold vehicles and trailers over a wide area. Here in the early sixties is GSU's own Bedford TK tractor unit delivering a new automatic coupling flat trailer to Fred Snaylam Transport in nearby Bolton. The telephone exchange for GSU was LONgford, Manchester (not LONdon as might be supposed). The tractor is a nominal 4-ton unit as it was solely used to collect new trailers from Scammell's in Watford and deliver them around the North West. The tractor unit would often visit the Watford factory three times a week to pick up trailers.

The Calico Printers Association operated within England's north west cotton belt. The association, originally established in 1899, comprised a vertically integrated set of cotton mills and dyers able to supply customers with their exact requirements. The 6-ton Scammell Scarab shown here was used for inter-mill transport and is fitted with flashing indicators above the cab roof. The theory of placing the indicators that high was to ensure that following traffic could see which way the unit was turning even if the trailer was not fitted with indicators.

As mentioned within the text, the undercarriage of the Scammell coupling fitted to the trailers was a relatively complex component with lots of moving parts. This meant that wear could take place and as a result GSU built up a substantial business in rebuilding the undercarriages, as can be established from this photograph.

A magnificent coal wagon! The combination of a Scammell Four-Trak four-in-line trailer and an Atkinson's (of Clitheroe) bulker combined to make a vehicle which could bag domestic coal at the delivery point or transfer coal by an inbuilt conveyor to underground cellars. The pairing of four-in-line trailer and Scammell automatic coupling was fairly unusual, normally these trailers had fifth wheel couplings.

What a sad little vehicle this was. Designated as the Scarab Four, it comprised a Leyland 20 (originally Standard Atlas) chassis/cab front end attached to a slightly modified Scarab/Townsman chassis rear end. It was designed as a 4-wheel alternative to the 3-wheel Scarab, but was not a success. The Karrier Bantam and the forthcoming Ford D Series Baby Artic were far better vehicles and only just over 100 of these Scarab 4 were built with the majority going to the South African Railways. A contemporary road test of these vehicles described the very poor vision from the cab, the large doors making egress difficult in restricted areas, difficulty in putting one's head out of the window when reversing and, most damagingly, the awful mechanical noise when travelling at any reasonable speed.

The modified automatic coupling that was designed by Mr Black (Senior) was taken up by the Ford Company for their 500 Series lorries and by Guy in Wolverhampton. Here is an advertisement extolling the virtues of the new coupling. It certainly looks a great deal simpler than the equivalent Scammell design, but it probably came into the market too late to make a big impact on sales of the Scammell version, which is a pity as the concept was very sound.

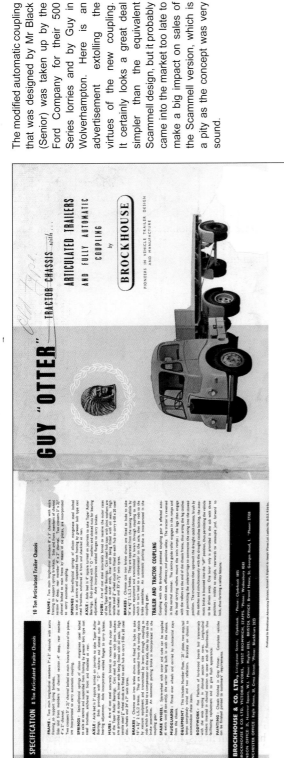

A Leyland Group Show possibly in Blackpool in 1964. On show, are two articulated LAD cabbed Leyland tractor units, two Scammell fifth wheel platform trailers, the unfortunate Scarab 4, based on a Standard Atlas, a 24ft automatic coupling trailer and a six ton Scammell Scarab three-wheel tractor. Behind the Scammell units is an aluminium-bodied Scammell trailer built by Bonallack called, quite delightfully, a Weightsaver.

The Grimsby Ice Company were one of the final users of the original design of Mechanical Horse, but shown here is fleet number 12, the only 6-ton Scammell Scarab to be used by the Ice Company. Loading the ice was fairly straightforward, but discharging the granulated ice into the trawler holds was an entirely different matter, The replacement for the Scammell's for transporting the ice to the trawlers came in the form of second-hand Guy Big J mobile concrete mixers. *(Courtesy Grimsby Ice Company)*

When the British Railways Sundries Division was transferred away from direct railway control into the National Freight Corporation, it was renamed National Carriers and gradually moved away from the use of rail services to road trunking between depots. Whilst in railway control the operation made great use of articulation with automatic coupling tractors and trailers, but operational necessities required an increasing use of rigid vehicles. Despite this change in operations articulated units continued on delivery and collection work throughout the 1970s as depicted here by a rather battered Ford D Series, seen in Leigh, Lancashire in 1978.

Amongst the last batches of Ford D Series tractor units fitted with 6-ton couplings and purchased by National Carriers was this model seen in Scarborough in 1981. National Carriers were the denationalised British Railways Sundries Division who transported items generally weighing less than 1-ton.

The Scottish Connection

One of the lesser known examples of improving the breed was the innovative automatic coupling which was marketed by J Brockhouse & Company Ltd of Clydebank in Scotland. This company was able to build and market a modified automatic coupling designed by the highly respected Senior Body Design Engineer of the SMT Sales and Service Company in Edinburgh. The gentleman was Mr Drummond Black Snr and SMT were the Bedford and Scammell distributors for central Scotland. Mr Black was an engineer of the old school, able to build scale models, an excellent body designer and an innovative engineer. He saw the various shortcomings of the basic Scammell coupling and set about designing out the intrinsic faults.

The most obvious problem to overcome was to ensure that the revised coupling was 'Fail Safe'. During his years as an engineer at SMT he came across many examples where the Scammell coupling did not fulfil its original ideals and the coupling did not work as planned. Invariably, this happened when the coupling had not been regularly greased and when uncoupled from the tractor unit the coupling remained in its 'folded' position and the front of the trailer fell ungracefully to the floor, requiring the services of a crane or hydraulic jacks to lift the front end of the trailer and straighten out the coupling.

An additional problem with the original Scammell design was the need for the driver to leave the cab to apply or release the trailer handbrake. Often, regular drivers would not worry with the trifle of applying the trailer handbrake and either the trailer would run away down a slope or possibly follow the tractor unit as it drove away. Alternatively, the next driver when trying to couple to the trailer would find the trailer moving away from him!

The other perceived shortcoming was the need for the removal of the rear cross member of the tractor chassis, leaving the regular converted tractors to flex more than they should and therefore cause excess wear and potential safety issues. Of course, the reason for the cross member removal was to allow the trailer undercarriage to connect easily with the tractor portion of the coupling.

The revision designed by Mr Black was to ensure that no modification was necessary to the tractor unit, thereby ensuring that the chassis remained fully standard.

The tractor portion of the coupling consisted of a complete kit which could be mounted directly on top of the existing chassis, thereby retained the complete rear chassis cross member. The coupling runners looked rather like a pair of closely spaced curved snow skis and the trailer locking system was fairly straightforward.

The trailer undercarriage was designed to be far simpler than its older brother, the main undercarriage struts were one piece and built to pivot through almost 90°. Instead of small flanged wheels to roll up the tractor ramps, a small horizontally mounted wheel ran between the tractor ramps, which were more closely spaced than those on the equivalent Scammell design.

The trailer handbrake was automatically disengaged or engaged as the trailer was uncoupled, with no need for the driver to take part in this operation. This meant there was little possibility of the trailer running away. And, just like the Scammell design, the electrical and brake connections between tractor and trailer were made automatically.

This new design of automatic coupling was manufactured by Brockhouse and taken up enthusiastically by Ford for use with the Fordson Thames 500 Series truck range. Since the coupling did not need any modifications to the chassis, Ford were able to use a standard tipper chassis for use with the coupling. Interestingly, prior to 1957, relatively few Ford chassis had been fitted with Scammell couplings and no doubt Ford management saw this as a way into a new market. (The date 1957 is significant since that year saw the introduction of the Trader chassis which could be modified for the fitment of a Scammell coupling).

Quite how popular the Brockhouse automatic coupling was is hard to say. Certainly, those fleets with existing Scammell couplings in use would not purchase an incompatible coupling system. However, the introduction of the Brockhouse coupling in 1953 was fortuitous in that many 'own account' operators were turning towards the articulation concept as a way to increase productivity. Since these operators generally only had small fleets, there would be no incompatibility problems, and no doubt this would be the market that Ford, and later Guy Motors, would approach.

Somewhat later Mr Drummond Black was to

apply the Scammell automatic coupling principle to a range of demountable 'swap' bodies to be used in conjunction with rigid chassis. These bodies generally boasted a separate subframe with legs which could be lowered to the ground to enable the body to stand on its own and for the rigid chassis to be moved from underneath the body.

Although demountable bodies were not a new idea, none of the early designs could be described as 'user friendly'. All required a fair amount of effort from the driver to pull or push recalcitrant legs out from the body and the body lock release mechanism, and, indeed, the raising of the body to allow the legs to drop was difficult prior to the general adoption of air suspension on the vehicle axles.

What Mr Black did was to make the demountable operation fully automatic, by the use of over-centre cams to lift the body and automatic lowering or raising of the landing legs, based exactly on the same principles as the original Scammell and later Brockhouse trailer couplings. Undoubtedly, a huge improvement on any existing demountable designs, and indeed a design that had huge potential, it was popular in certain areas and was manufactured by Davies Magnet of Ware in conjunction with Adrolic Engineering of East Kilbride. It was marketed as the Davies Automount Swop Body System. Davies Magnet were recognised as manufacturing a high quality fifth wheel coupling, whilst Adrolic are best know for the 'Anti-Jackknife' device which was based on a steel hydraulic ram fitted above chassis level between the tractor and trailer and reducing potential severe oscillation.

In addition to the design of new coupling devices, Mr Black was an enthusiastic developer of better bodies for specific trades. One item which springs to mind was the requirement for the safe transport of hanging meat. Since hanging meat meant a high centre of gravity for the vehicle, a danger given the poor state of the roads and the numerous tight curves on some main roads, the lower the meat could hang, the safer the vehicle.

Mr Black used a Scammell drop-frame trailer chassis as the base for a meat carrier, but instead of just using the roof to suspend the hanging meat rails from, he designed what could best be described as an integral body with the roof rails directly attached to the chassis, with the body having no load carrying requirements, its cladding used to purely to protect the load.

Again, apart from relatively local purchases Mr Black's designs do not seem to have had any major effect on the main United Kingdom vehicle, though alternative demountable systems are still being built today. Of course, with modern warehousing/handling techniques, less time is being taken loading the majority of lorries in use today and there is less need for bodies to be loaded apart from their chassis. However, one wonders that if Mr Black had been based in Lancashire, Birmingham or London whether the designs would have really taken off…. One can but surmise.

However, it is always instructive to consider how dedicated, forward-looking engineers can always improve the breed.

There have always been inventions which revolutionised the haulage business, pneumatic tyres and the diesel engine being just two of the earlier ones. To those one could add the advent of palletisation, and the introduction of the curtain-side trailer, both of which have helped the driver in his work. The invention of the automatic coupling did more than just increase the load carrying capacity of a fleet, it improved productivity and versatility at a stroke and at the time was a major step forward in the modernisation of road haulage.

As noted above there are a number of automatic coupling tractors (both three- and four-wheel) and their respective trailers in preservation. There is a club catering for enthusiasts of this unique concept, which was formed in 1983 and brought together a number of like-minded enthusiasts who had been exchanging notes for some time. A bi-monthly magazine is issued, and this covers the latest information on vehicle movements, discovery of hitherto unknown horses in scrap yards, vehicles, trailers and spares for sale and wanted, as well as special features, rally reports, articles and photographs. They are the Mechanical Horse Club, and can be contacted via the membership secretary:

John Nuttall,
77, St. Asaph Road,
Dyserth,
Denbighshire. LL18 6HG

The dairy companies across the country made great use of the Scammell automatic couplings in their milk distribution operations. As the railway companies had found the rapid exchange of empty and loaded trailers really simplified what today would be called the logistics of milk supply. This particular scene was captured at the Didsbury (Manchester) dairy of Healds Dairies Ltd.

Postscript

Learning to drive the three-wheeler articulated tractors was a difficult job, or to be precise, reversing was impossible until the knack was learnt. The Railway Companies had their own training schools, but as staff shortages arose in the fifties many railway 'other ranks' were pressed into service after the minimum amount of training. Perhaps the reminiscences of Mr R Harris will suffice to explain the problems. He joined British Railways at Brighton in 1964 as a porter, but rapidly progressed to driving rigid vehicles. He was soon given the opportunity to try his hand at driving both Scarabs and Bantams. His first comment about the Scarab was that if you did not notice the position of the front wheel when approaching the vehicle, then when you let the clutch in you had the disconcerting sensation of going sideways if the steering had been left on full lock. For several weeks Mr Harris practised reversing the trailer, which, of course, had a mind of its own. He continues, "I remember one day reversing the trailer end on to a rail wagon, the rear of the trailer swung round straight up to the doors, dead square, tractor in line, perfect. The fact was that it wasn't against the wagon I had intended was beside the point!"

Perhaps the final comment on the automatic coupling system should come from the first edition of the Scammell Mechanical Horse handbook, which states:

"Owing to the low first cost, low maintenance charges and extreme manoeuvrability, the horse has hitherto been considered economically indispensable for short distance collection, delivery and haulage work.

The motor lorry and light delivery van displaced the horse from many fields, but a vehicle of entirely special design was needed to equal the horse drawn van in all its good points, while yet retaining the obvious advantages of a mechanically propelled vehicle as compared with the horse.

Such a vehicle has now been produced, the SCAMMELL MECHANICAL HORSE, and it now combines all the merits of the horse with the advantages of the motor vehicle in increased carrying capacity and higher speed. In the development of this vehicle a further point of great importance has emerged, for it is found that this machine can do more efficiently and more economically much of the work at present done by the motor lorry".

That comment could hardly be bettered, the Mechanical Horse not only replaced the horse, but brought the principle of articulation to the transport industry, where that form of transportation now reigns supreme.

For a long period Roadline (the parcels operation of British Road Services) operated a large fleet of Bedford TK tractor units often coupled to 28ft long box vans for the collection and delivery of parcels traffic. This typical combination is seen at the Hull factory of Humbrol of plastic kits and model paints fame.

A Ford D Series with Scammell coupling seen in Trafford Park, Manchester.

The works fleet of Scammell Motors included a number of automatic coupling articulated units for spares delivery as typified by this Leyland Boxer seen near Cardiff Road power station in Watford in 1978.